The BIG DAY

JoJo PUBLISHING

Wendy Bull

The Big Day — Weddings: Wicked, Wonderful and Wild
Wendy Bull

Published by JoJo Publishing
First published 2012

'Yarra's Edge'
2203/80 Lorimer Street
Docklands VIC 3008
Australia

Email: jo-media@bigpond.net.au or visit www.jojopublishing.com

© Wendy Bull

All rights reserved. No part of this printed or video publication may be reproduced, stored in or introduced into a retrieval system, or transmitted, in any form, or by any means (electrical, mechanical, photocopying, recording or otherwise) without the prior written permission of the publisher and copyright owner.

JoJo Publishing

Editor: Ormé Harris
Designer / typesetter: Chameleon Print Design
Printed in Singapore by KHL Printing

National Library of Australia Cataloguing-in-Publication data

Author:	Bull, Wendy.
Title:	The big day : weddings : wicked, wonderful and wild / Wendy Bull.
ISBN:	9780987192752 (pbk.)
Subjects:	Bull, Wendy--Career in weddings.
	Marriage celebrants--Australia--Anecdotes.
	Weddings--Australia--Humor.
Dewey Number:	392.50207

About the Author

Wendy Bull is one of Sydney's leading Civil Marriage Celebrants and since 1995 has officiated at thousands of weddings for local, interstate and overseas couples. Prior to becoming a fulltime celebrant, Wendy's career was in sales and marketing across a diverse range of industries and after achieving numerous and necessary qualifications, she went on to teach and train for nine years at private business colleges and in the TAFE system in Business Studies, Communication and Management. She has also published many business articles in magazines and on-line. Wendy is a wonderful raconteur and public speaker and has also given radio, television and many community presentations. This skill has proven to be an asset in Wendy's work as a celebrant. All cultures are embraced in her work and she offers not only legal civil marriages, but many cultural and religious, naming, commitment and renewal of marriage vows ceremonies. She writes and performs a wide range of personalised ceremonies to suit individual needs and all occasions.

Wendy's storytelling shines in this collection of mostly hilarious, sometimes challenging, experiences from her many years as a Civil Celebrant.

Dedication

For Philip, my long-suffering and patient 'Roadie'

Acknowledgements

I would like to thank Philip, my wonderful Roadie, without whom I would be unable to do this work I love and who has been supportive of my dream throughout the writing of this book. My gratitude also goes to Barry Dorr of JoJo Publishing for believing in me, Ormé Harris, my Editor, for her wise words of wisdom and Phil Smith, author and friend, for his endearing encouragement and love of alliterations.

Table of Contents

About the Author iii

Acknowledgements vii

Chapter 1   Breasts 1

Chapter 2   The Glam, Gorgeous and Ghastly 11

Chapter 3   Aspirations 33

Chapter 4   An Attack of the Vapours 71

Chapter 5   Keeping up Appearances 85

Chapter 6   Bloody Liars and Thieves 107

Chapter 7   Location, Location, Location 125

Chapter 8   Stir Fry 149

Chapter 9   Names 171

Chapter 10   The Big Day 181

Chapter 1
Breasts

Enormous Triple E's hung from Melanie's chest and, resembling the pointy peaks of the Sydney Opera House, they arrived before she did, down the windy path in the beautiful Royal Botanic Gardens. Melanie stole the limelight in her brilliant white gown with its hugely false diamante, bling-encrusted bodice; her four equally attractive and voluptuously breasted bridesmaids followed on behind.

That she had arrived before the appointed time came as no real surprise — the sooner the ceremony was finished the better and then they could all start getting into the grog.

But Melanie's dad, Trev, was already half-tanked from a morning down at the local and putting a bit on the dogs — couldn't wait for his daughter's arrival — and, reeking of week-old alcohol at best, sidled up to me and slurred, 'Wait 'til you see 'er in 'er frock; them big tits will be pushed up like you wouldn't believe — we call 'er Melons, y'know. Melanie, Melons — get it?'

And trying to whisper as quietly as his alcoholic condition would allow, he finished by saying, 'Takes after th' missus!' Not surprisingly, Melanie's mother, Gloria, had overheard and obviously not sharing the same sentiments as Trev swung around towards him, her equally massive breasts arriving before her face did and before the rest of her slim and attractive body.

The angry face of Gloria spat back at Trev saying, 'Shut ya friggin' face, ya stupid ol' fart.'

Much to the amusement of the guests and the ogling groomsmen, Trev couldn't help himself: 'Big tits; honestly Gloria, after 28 years in the nest, that's all ya got goin' for ya.'

There was no getting away from it. Melanie had always known her tits would be her dowry and her insurance for a most financially secure and sexually fulfilled married life. It then occurred to me why Melanie hadn't wanted Trev to walk her up the aisle and 'give her away'. Melanie knew her dad would start on about the tits again and he and Gloria would be at it like dogs with a bone. 'The quicker we get out of here,' Melanie whispered to me after signing the marriage register, as she heaved herself up to stand behind her breasts, 'the quicker we can catch up to Dad's level.'

* * *

Victoria's breasts too, were indeed to her advantage and decorated with much elegance, just like her double-tiered wedding cake. Her breasts fitted beautifully into the bodice of her elegant wedding gown. Victoria was an absolute stunner there was no getting away from it and the few boyfriends she'd had along the way towards the altar had managed to persuade the religious and devout Victoria that her breasts would indeed be her life-long asset. They felt good; they looked good. They were generously rounded with an impressive cleavage. These breasts were definitely on display — after all, it was her 'Big Day' and Victoria was going to make the most of it.

'You look stunning, Victoria,' I commented as I met her by the bridal car. 'You look absolutely stunning.' But while Victoria was the confident, glamorous bride, her groom was quite the opposite.

Noah stood at the top of the aisle tightly clenching his hands; his small, pale face wore the look of sheer terror; perhaps he wasn't sure what he was supposed to do with the beautiful breasts after the wedding was over. I could see his armpits start to look moist. His eyes were double-glazed and fixed as a kitchen sink upon the sight of the approaching Victoria and her magnificent breasts. He'd been a 'good boy' and come from a conservative, religious home just as Victoria had. 'A perfect match made in heaven,' the grey-headed mothers had whispered from beneath their fluttering headscarves.

Despite the gathering rain clouds the ceremony was progressing well and as I declared the beautiful Victoria and the nervous Noah, 'husband and wife' the first crack of lightning struck. As I quickly instructed the groom to 'kiss the bride' and then make a dash for the marquee, Noah's nerves got the better of him and not wanting to miss 'The Kiss' he lunged forward towards the beautiful Victoria with his lips puckered together like the tight end of a birthday balloon, his eyes screwed tightly shut.

As the first spats of rain started to fall, Noah, wanting to embrace the moment as well as his bride, flung his arms around the beautiful Victoria's elegant neck. But just as he did so, he began to faint and as his knees became increasingly weaker his legs buckled beneath him and he started falling to the ground. As he slid down, trying to regain some sort of consciousness, his fingers curled and hooked over the front of the beautiful Victoria's diamante encrusted bodice and grasping at her breasts he tried in vain to keep in control. But with Noah's fingers hooked over the top of Victoria's bodice and as he attempted one last ditched effort to regain his composure, he blacked out and fell heavily down into a heap.

Suddenly out popped Victoria's breasts from the bodice of her dress, perfectly poised for the occasion, pointing straight forward towards the 150 horrified guests and the two delighted photographers. Shocked that Noah would have fainted at the mere thought of a kiss, Victoria threw down her bouquet and fell to her knees over the poor pale-faced Noah as he lay peacefully in a dead faint upon the soft green grass.

With a quick glance around, Victoria noticed the videographer going into fast action, aiming at the beautiful breasts pointing out over the top of her frock, and as she vainly tried to stuff them back inside the beaded bodice, she turned and screamed: 'Turn that fucking thing off — can't you see we have a situation here?'

As Victoria's breasts swayed from left to right in the breeze and with large drops of rain splattering their way across her fine chest, she furiously fanned her free hand over Noah's face and continued by pleading, 'Oh don't die Noah, well not just yet, anyway!' 'He's OK, Victoria,' I said trying to calm her as I pushed the wet legal papers into my briefcase. 'He'll come round in a moment.'

Without a backward glance and quickly grabbing the microphone, I asked the 150 guests to proceed across to the marquee for tea and sandwiches before the heavens opened. And as the devout, grey headed, scarfed ladies flapped their way off across the grass with the sound of Victoria's expletives still ringing in their ears, I could not help but notice the bemused look on the videographer's face. Working now in total frenzy like two deranged madmen, the photographer and videographer kept clicking and whirring away, all in the name of getting the perfect footage of the beautiful Victoria and the sumptuous breasts. Then looking up in sheer panic, Victoria yelled, 'Wendy, they *will* edit all that out, won't they; you know, the word 'fuck' and all that?' 'Oh yes Victoria,' I replied with as straight a face as I could muster, 'of course they will.' Sneaking a quick glance across at the amused videographer, I was instantly convinced that no such editing would occur and a most pleasurable night would be had by all in the dark room. Breasts, tits, knockers — call them what you will, one way or another, they always seemed to entertain.

* * *

It only stood to reason that with the new fashions of the Wonderbra and the U line bra, cleavages had made a healthy come-back into fashion and for that, many a male would be eternally grateful. Biggest was best. 'The Big Day' often had nothing to do with the day itself; it was more often than not, all about the tits. 'Big tits are good,' sighed one best man, 'and the bigger the better.' And while we waited for the bride to arrive, he raised his half-empty stubby towards his mouth and spluttered: 'Tits, Wendy; just can't do without 'em.' Nothing had ever prepared me for the amusements of breasts in the world of weddings; never did I think that breasts would generate such interest and that they would amuse so endlessly. It prompted the verbal and breasts could instantly delight the eye of a groomsman or guest and create so many wonderful and interesting scenarios. Breasts have a way of turning the most dignified and formal celebration into a videographer's delight, and I was always standing close enough to hear their comments as the bride walked up the aisle.

Breasts of course come in all shapes and sizes, and especially at weddings, delight the guests in a variety of situations and in a myriad of ways but never was I so astounded to see the heaving and bulging breasts of a 57-year-old pink fairy. Surrounded by over 100 elegant and very well-heeled guests and frock-coated groomsmen at an exclusive resort in the Southern Highlands, we were waiting for the bride to make her entrance so the ceremony could commence. As I glanced across the meticulously manicured lawns, I saw a bright pink figure, arms waving, thundering towards me.

Coming closer into view, I saw a woman with the hugest breasts — like enormous, pink, hot air balloons — heaving from side to side. Astoundingly, she was dressed as a pink fairy. A tiny, pink ballet tutu just covered her thick and dimply thighs and as she ran, she frantically waved a sparkling, silver wand. A tiny, silver tiara was perched atop of her bright red, frizzy hair. 'Wendy, Wendy,' I heard her call as she came rushing up to me, right through the middle of the guests and up to the end of the red-carpeted aisle where I stood waiting with the groom. 'I am so glad I've caught up with you, I've wanted to meet you now for ages.'

The look of amazement on such well-heeled guests at a five star resort, clutching their glasses of champagne, had to be seen to be believed.

'I'm Beth,' the big, fat, pink fairy gasped, her breasts heaving up and down and her long, glittery earrings dangling like Buddhist wind chimes onto her shoulders. 'I'm the 'Pink Fairy'. Do you want a magic fairy at your wedding today? I do weddings. People can make special wishes and I will wave my magic wand like star dust and all their wishes will come true.'

The big, pink fairy, who glistened from top to toe with pink, spray-on, sparkly glitter, stood panting heavily and beaming broadly towards the guests.

'Beth,' I said thinking quickly, 'I don't think we need a pink fairy at *this* wedding but how about you leave your business card and I'll call you later?' With her silver wand in her left hand, Beth plunged her spare right hand deeply down into the cleavage of her bulging hot air balloons and extracted a small, crumpled pack of business cards.

I smiled a 'thank you' trying to get her to disappear but she stood fast, beaming again towards the guests. 'Anyone of youse want to make a wish then?' she called out. Suddenly, the guests draped in fashion's finest, burst into loud applause as Beth thundered around in a circle waving her silver wand, breasts heaving and plunging, much to their amusement.

Thankfully, Beth took the hint and disappeared as quickly as she had come, waving the so-called magic silver wand, her mighty legs thumping off behind the trimmed, mazed hedges.

* * *

Breasts too, are also meant for breastfeeding, even at weddings and many a screaming baby can only be quietened by a soft, warm breast and an endless supply of its mother's milk. Again, the soft, voluptuous mounds are eagerly gazed upon as they are

Chapter 1 — *Breasts*

gently extracted from the bra and plunged into the mouth of the hungry child. It is now not uncommon for the 'cool' mum to have her 'child' with her at the wedding and all her friends with their $2,000 strollers lined up for the occasion. I can usually and instantly predict a few disruptions and after enquiring about the number and type of guests attending the ceremony, have often suggested that couples put on their wedding invitations 'adults only please'. To this very day and for the life of me, I can never understand why a young couple can't organise a baby-sitter when they attend a wedding, even just to give themselves a break and enjoy the day, but they never seem to and over the years I have just learnt to carry on regardless.

Predictably, the minute the quietness reigns and the ceremony starts, you can count on a startled baby, not used to the sudden quiet and lack of attention, letting rip with a brain-piercing screech — just like breasts, sure attention-getters.

But Kylie the bride, with her baby Zak in tow, was having none of this noisy baby drama at *her* wedding — babies either shut up or got fed. Zak got fed.

With the ceremony just starting, Zak, who up to this time had been quite content to gurgle away in his baby stroller, suddenly let out the obligatory screech. 'Shut up Zak,' hissed Kylie again, clutching her bouquet tightly, waiting to get married, 'just wait 'til the vows are over.'

But dear little Zak wanted immediate attention and continued the screech. 'Wendy, you'll have to wait,' interrupted Kylie as she pushed her bouquet into my hands and rushing forward, grabbed Zak out of his stroller, 'Zak'll need to be fed.'

So while I clutched onto my microphone with one hand and Kylie's bouquet in the other, she reached for the screaming Zak and plonking herself down in the front row alongside the guests, extracted her wet, left breast from her wedding dress and shoved it down into Zak's screeching, little mouth.

The guests waited and stared while Kylie tried in vain to feed Zak but today Zak decided he wasn't in any hurry, so Kylie very keen to become the 'lawful wedded wife' jumped up and standing again beside the groom said, 'Carry on Wendy, let's get the vows over and done with.' So I carried on with the ceremony and was finally able to declare the happy couple 'husband and wife' while Zak hung firmly on to Kylie's left breast for fear of being put back to bed on his mother's wedding day.

And whilst you wouldn't think vows and breasts have much in common, I can assure you, they have. Breasts have an awful lot to do with a marriage proposal and invariably, both brides and breasts end up at the altar.

Even five star weddings in five star locations can't escape the breasts. About to perform a ceremony inside a five star Sydney hotel, the guests sipping their chilled 'champagne on arrival' freebie, I spotted a young elegantly attired mother open the front of her frock and start to breastfeed in full view of all the staff and guests. They say a hotel professional doesn't miss a trick and quietly a well-meaning attendant slid up to the breastfeeding guest and asked, 'Would Madam prefer to feed her baby in a private adjoining room?' 'Certainly not,' retorted the slightly greying, 40-year-old Generation Y breastfeeding mother glaring back at him. 'I'm perfectly happy here thank you — and I'm *not* a Madam,' she continued loudly, 'and I *do* have a name.' Sometimes even the most well-trained hotel attendant just can't win.

* * *

But still many a bride still doesn't seem to have heard of the Wonderbra or declines to wear one. Many Double and Triple E's have hung down against the bride's rib-cage like deflated, stretched hot water bottles and sadly, it's not a good look especially when the dress neckline plunges down to the waist. A U line bra would make so much difference and give it some extra uplifting sex appeal to say the least. It's not often a matter of not being able to afford an expensive bra — breasts big and small can be squashed and uplifted into the cheapest of brands, it's just that some brides don't do the obvious and take a good look at themselves in the mirror from all angles before the so-called Big Day. A sidelong glance across at the bride often reveals the sad lack of a decent fitting bra and can certainly ruin the look of a pretty enough bride who has gone to every trouble to look her best in other areas. A photographer once whispered to me, 'Look Wendy, nice tits but shame about the bra; an old pair of men's braces would've done the trick.'

And so I witnessed the endless array of odd and different shaped and sized breasts which seemed to pop up or come out of everywhere on The Big Day. They really did look like the massive, pointy peaks of the Sydney Opera House which I stared at hundreds of times during weddings, and they didn't disappoint the groomsmen or photographers, who generally always seemed to have an eye for such detail.

Chapter 2
The Glam, Gorgeous and Ghastly

From ugly ducklings into swans, perhaps there was such a thing as a 'big pink fairy magic wand', as many times over I could hardly recognise the bride on her wedding day. From visiting my office as real ugly ducklings in jeans and T-shirt they would turn into fairy princesses on their 'Big Day'.

From floppy hot water bottles into Opera Houses, I witnessed it all, always to the great amusement of the groomsmen.

The movie *Muriel's Wedding* encouraged many a bride to turn herself from an ugly duckling into a swan, even if it was only just for a day.

Danni came to see me, openly admitting she never thought she was good enough to get married until Damien came along and popped the question one Saturday afternoon, after he'd been on his back under the car fixing the muffler. So Damien covered in grease, down on one knee and with a can of Tooheys to steady his nerves and gain some Dutch courage, had proposed to Danni.

Danni also admitted she loved the movie, *Muriel's Wedding*. As she passed my bookcase on the way out of my office, her eye caught my DVD selection. 'Can I borrow that?' she asked. 'Of course,' I said thinking she wanted to grab a hint or two.

Danni had grabbed more than a hint or two and arrived most confidently on the Big Day in a big stretch limo. This wasn't the shy little Danni who had visited in her jeans and T-shirt; it was obvious she'd had a few champagnes for the Dutch courage to kick in. Danni emerged as the confident bride and brushing the waiting crowd aside, she swept up into the bridal hall waving, and wrinkling her nose, at the same time offering the coy Princess Diana look from behind her fringe.

As she approached the start of the red carpeted aisle, and with Abba playing loudly 'I do, I do, I do,' I asked the guests to stand for the bride's entrance. Danni looked shyly out from under both her fringe and veil but I wasn't prepared for her stopping at the end of every pew to acknowledge the standing friends and family.

As she waved to her guests down one row she then turned and waved across down the other; then she'd take a slow step forward and repeat the whole process waving down each row until she reached the altar. The whole trip up the aisle took something like ten minutes as she wrinkled her nose at every stop — the slowest aisle walker I ever encountered.

Danni mimicked every 'Muriel wave and look', every step of the way Toni Collette's coy wedding-day style jumped across at me — Danni had had her own private rehearsal and this was how it was going to be.

She took her time over everything and even stopped to wave to the guests between the vows and the ring ceremony, again wrinkling her nose in true Muriel fashion. Danni was on show big-time and at the end of the ceremony responding to a huge round of applause for such a dramatic presentation, she left the groom's side and rushed up to my microphone. Grabbing it from me, she yelled into it with her loud, hoarse voice: 'Youse are all now welcome to come and get stuck into the grog.' Dragging Damien by the hand she tore off down the aisle, heading towards the bar and waving the photographer aside who was waiting to go out into the garden for photos. She yelled, 'And youse can wait too, youse bloody photographers!'

But unfortunately for Danni she didn't see the buckle in the end of the red carpet, and in her haste to get to the bar, tripped and fell with one almighty thud, taking poor Damien down with her.

Chapter 2 — *The Glam, Gorgeous and Ghastly*

Lying flat on her face with Damien sprawled amongst the mounds of white fluff, Danni turned her head and yelled, 'Well come on youse guys, help us up.' The three groomsmen bent to help poor Danni and Damien to their feet but as Danni weighed in at a massive 140 kilos, it took a few heaves to get her standing and back onto her feet. Metres of white satin and lace had twisted itself all around her waist and the blue bridal garter delightfully showed itself stretched tight above the knee, waiting for the obligatory alcoholic teeth extraction later in the evening on the dance floor. The dress had to be gathered up and smoothed out, and after adjusting her veil, the unfazed Danni continued to the bar.

The guests were quick to gather around knocking back as many drinks as they could manage with Danni enjoying every minute of the attention. But Damien, not to miss out on the limelight, jumped up on to the top of the bar and called for quiet.

'You know,' he said beaming broadly and winking across at the best man, 'Danni always said she wanted to get me into bed on the wedding night, plain cold bloody sober but she's got two chances now, mate — none and Buckley's.'

Damien was in his element standing on the bar; all eyes in the room were on him. 'Shit,' he continued beaming broadly. 'But I didn't think youse'd be in such a hurry to get the dress up over ya knickers, Danni,' he yelled staring down at his bride. 'You didn't have to trip over a bloody piece of red carpet, to get ya fucking frock off ya know; ya only had to ask.'

The crowd roared and whistled and I could tell Danni didn't mind one bit. She'd got her man to the altar and that was that.

I felt like saying, 'Geez, you're terrible Muriel,' but I kept that comment to myself.

* * *

Marriage is often about just wanting to be a princess for a day: the white fluff, champagne and heaps of attention. Forget the future

13

— what's that? The walk along the red carpet was probably the only time they could pretend to be on Sydney's very exclusive A list.

Of course it's the dress and invariably the breasts that steal the limelight even more than the bride. Everyone knew what Trish was like but the dress nearly caused an instant divorce. As Trish Taylor stepped out of the Rolls, her eyes on the cameras, her right foot went right into the middle of a pile of doggy poo and despite all the scraping and sole cleaning efforts from the wedding car driver, the foul smell hung around in the mid-Summer heat. 'First time I've ever been asked to clean the bloody bride's shoes,' the driver had whispered to me. 'First and fucking last time too, that's for sure.'

Trish had tried to impress me at every meeting with what the Taylors owned: the share portfolios, the cruiser on the harbour, the country property and so the list dragged on but quite frankly I didn't much care about the Taylors, simply because I didn't care much for the Taylors' daughter. Not one little bit. The whole wedding event was about 'me and my dress' and about the endless family wealth.

She was such an awful bore and how her poor groom-to-be and some of those other poor to-be-pitied grooms fell for the whole wedding catastrophe, I am yet to fully understand. She had told me, 'Wait 'til you see my dress, it's simply divine.' Wait I did, but not with the same amount of enthusiasm as Trish. Not by a long shot.

Taronga Park Zoo doesn't always emit the most pleasant of smells and Trish's entrance in 'the dress' did not steal the show as hoped; the vile stench from her shoe, which followed Trish's huge and fleshy frame as she limped up the aisle, did not come from the elephants.

Metres of flowing fabric surrounded Trish's frame, a large billowing mass of stark white with her breasts squashed tightly into the formidable bodice like two large Queensland Bottle Trees up for auction.

Chapter 2 — *The Glam, Gorgeous and Ghastly*

There was nothing particularly spectacular about the dress, except that it was the hugest number I had ever seen. It resembled a reception marquee you'd see at Oaks Day at Randwick: an enormous white mound, billowing in the breeze, just metres and metres of bright white fluff and with not a sequin in sight.

The ghastly smell which came from Trish's shoe drew attention from the guests in the front row but we carried on regardless.

I could see Trish trying to catch my eye as I read the ceremony wording and at one stage I caught her pointing to her dress — I was in for a costly surprise.

The ceremony over and coping with the dreadful doggy poo odour, the bridesmaids and I all helped seat Trish at the signing table, tucking some of her dress beneath. Of course it didn't all fit, so the second third we draped over the back of the chair on which she sat and the final third across over the groom's lap. In the middle of it sat Trish with her bulbous breasts proudly displayed.

Trish had chosen a red and white theme for her wedding. The bridesmaids carried bouquets of blood-red roses and the groomsmen all wore red rose buttonholes. Red candles flickered on the table, their wax already melting down the sides and sticking fast to the white, linen table cloth.

Having only slightly recovered from the doggy poo on her white satin shoes and with the wedding ring firmly on her finger, she looked up me and asked, 'Wendy, Wendy do you like my dress?' 'Trish it's gorgeous,' I replied. 'Well, come on, guess what it cost?' she asked excitedly, looking up from the Marriage Register. Without being prompted, or waiting for my answer, and so that all the guests could hear, she said in the loudest and politest voice she could muster, 'It cost $12,000.'

'Fuck!' exclaimed the groom tightly clutching the signing pen and probably realising his sudden error at marrying a girl who would even *think* about spending $12,000 on a dress. '$12,000?' he spluttered. 'Christ, Trish; what about the bloody mortgage?'

15

'Oh *fuck* the bloody mortgage,' retorted Trish loudly, as the guests waited for the unfolding row. 'A girl *spoils* herself on her wedding day, anyway, what with dog shit all over my shoes …'

Jumping up from her seat in the front row, the meticulously groomed Mrs Taylor came flying across to the pale-faced groom, her black and gold fascinator bobbing like a yacht on Sydney harbour. 'For Godsakes, Robert, be quiet; you've married Trish and that's that.' But as she swung around to console her snivelling daughter, her dainty, silver shoulder evening bag sailed around over the signing table and knocked over one of the dripping red wax candles, spraying hot red wax all down the front of Trish's $12,000 billowing marquee of a dress. 'Now look what you've done, you stupid old bitch,' Trish screamed at her mother as she jumped to her feet. 'It was *you* who told me to spend all the money on my dress in the first place and that Robert wouldn't mind — it's all your fault!'

With the bride continuing to snivel through her tears, we finished the signing after which Trish in her doggy-poo satin stilettos and the pale-faced Robert managing very forced smiles and, trying to keep up appearances, walked off down the aisle to pose for their bridal photos which were to be taken in the grounds of the zoo. I can assure you, doggy poo is one thing but red candle wax that doesn't ever come off anything is another.

Marriage candles are in a league all of their own, and damned if you can ever get them to light outside in the first place, even if they're inside a glass candle holder.

* * *

Julie just *had* to have a marriage candle — on the beach at high-tide, in the middle of a cold windy Autumn day. In fact Julie had to have seven candles, for the number of years she and the poor suffering groom had known each other and the candles were to be placed on the top of seven, small, moulded sand castles in front of the bride and groom. As directed by the bride, the

Chapter 2 — *The Glam, Gorgeous and Ghastly*

groomsmen had arrived an hour early to make the sandcastles and it was the best man's job to get down and light these just before the vows. However, a howling gale had whipped up in the meantime, and wiping sand from his eyes, the best man had no chance of even striking a match. Julie was insistent they be lit but try as he might it was a fruitless task as everyone could see.

The guests started to giggle and point, the poor best man down on his knees in the sand, striking match after match, in front of the seven little sand castles.

'For crying out loud,' yelled Julie through the howling gale, 'hurry up and light the bloody things!' But lighting candles under such conditions was an absolute impossibility. With time dragging on and Julie determined that the candles be lit, she hitched up her billowing wedding dress and knelt down in the soft sand beside the best man, before the seven castles with the seven marriage candles sticking out of the tops of the seven sandy turrets. But it wasn't until she herself attempted the impossible, did she dry her eyes and decide it was time to carry on with the ceremony. 'Fucking candles,' I heard the groom mutter. 'I never wanted the fucking things in the first place.' But Julie overheard him and rudely retorted in front of the giggling guests, 'Don't start bleating about the candles not being lit; you couldn't light a bloody barbecue if your arse was pointing to the griller plate.'

* * *

The whole wedding spectrum displayed itself in the most wonderful and colourful array of bridal wear. From T-shirts and jeans and casual sun frocks, to bridal gowns of tacky lime green to black, the latter, I must say, always made a nice change from white, creamy white, very creamy white, ivory, very ivory, light ivory, light champagne and champagne. What choices!

But nothing could beat the bright scarlet wedding dress which came floating down the path towards us one beautiful

17

Spring day. Both families, who made up the large contingent of Greek guests, lined the aisle in their smart Vicky Mar suits and frocks, the men in their dark ties and suits. Not an Orthodox Church wedding for these two.

It was the look of horror on about 100 faces that made my day, especially from the groom and family who had expected the bride-to-be in the traditional Greek virginal white. But not Gina — Gina wanted to make a statement, so, arriving in a huge scarlet red meringue and wearing a stark white veil in contrast, she approached the silent, waiting crowd.

'Holy fuck!' exclaimed the groom so loudly that not one of the guests missed hearing. 'Look at my fucking red bride!'

'Michael, she looks simply gorgeous,' I whispered trying to smooth over the situation and shut him up. 'Just look — Gina looks simply amazing.'

'But it's fucking red!' screamed Michael at the top of his voice. 'What the hell youse wearing fucking red for?' he threw at Gina as she arrived to stand beside him.

I didn't want to catch Gina's eye so I quickly started the ceremony while all the little Greek, Vicky Mar groomed ladies stood with looks of horror on their ashen faces, and the men tried to hide their amusement as they stood like little toy tin soldiers behind their wives.

But Michael wouldn't let up about the 'fucking red dress' and all through the ceremony he continued to admonish his bride. 'Bloody red, mate, holy fuck; what youse wearing fucking red for?' I could hear him asking her.

But poor Gina, who couldn't take any more berating, burst into loud sobs and cried all the way through the ceremony and spilled tears all over the marriage register as she signed her life away with Michael who hated the fucking red dress.

* * *

Chapter 2 — *The Glam, Gorgeous and Ghastly*

Ah … the Dress! What to wear on the 'Big Day' was always foremost in the bride's mind. Bridal magazines and books were always purchased by the volume, which made the newsagent a very happy man. The once new crisp and informative *Brides' Diary* and piles of wedding magazines, always ended up looking like a tatty pile of thumbed through 1958 *Geographics* generally to be found in the doctor's surgery.

'It's *got* to have a train,' would be the usual whimper from the bride in my office thumbing through bridal magazines. 'But I'm not telling you anything else,' they'd conclude as the groom listened in — all ears.

It was the unnecessary bridal train which always caused the most problems — apart from the breasts that is. You couldn't trip over a pair of Double E's but you sure could trip over a bridal train especially the Father of the Bride who would already have had a couple of drinks and be so absorbed in giving his daughter away that, as he turned away from the bride, his foot would land dead centre of the train, leaving a dirty big footprint for all to see. Dressmakers and bridal gown boutiques have a lot to answer for, telling brides they 'must' have a train.

A train is simply an added piece of material which hangs down the back of the dress, with no earthly use except making the dress more costly, getting in the way and becoming covered in grease as the bride emerges from the bridal car and squeezes past the old type vintage door lock. And trying to dance the bridal waltz is an absolute impossibility with a few metres of material sweeping along behind on the dance floor. Trains are a huge nuisance, especially on the dance floor where they are an outright hazard.

* * *

I occasionally felt very sorry for some brides who tried their utmost, like the poor humble Catherine. After producing three

The Big Day

absolutely beautiful children, Catherine and Tim decided it was time for the sanctity of marriage.

Attractive and pencil-slim Catherine was all excitement and had, according to her mother-in-law Marlene, stayed home for nine years, raising her three beautiful sons with every little bit of love and care she could possibly afford to provide, keeping a spotless home and living on the smell of an oily rag.

Prospective mother-in-law Marlene told me Catherine had gone shopping and chosen a gorgeous slim-line classic number to wear for her big day but Tim, as the bread-winner was mortified when he saw it, and decided his wife-to-be looked far too attractive as 'the men at the wedding might fancy her and her breasts' and therefore he did not approve. So he demanded she take the dress back and get a refund. He then drove her to a bridal-wear discount factory outlet and assisted her in choosing something 'more suitable for a mother of three boys' as he put it.

'Wait until you see what he chose,' Marlene confided to me on the phone. 'Poor Catherine, I am horrified to think he's making her wear it.' Catherine had had no say in the matter and that was that.

I looked forward to Catherine and Tim's special day but certainly not with the same enthusiasm as Tim, who told me proudly before Catherine arrived for the ceremony, *'I chose the dress.'*

As the music struck up, the beautiful Catherine made her appearance but outrageously decked out from head to toe in what I call an 'Oklahoma Number'. For over her shoulder she carried a white lacy parasol and perched on her head was the largest, whitest, flounciest hat I had ever seen.

Sadly, she wore a frock to match. It had huge, puffy leg o' mutton Princess Diana sleeves and a skirt as wide as the Oklahoma Plains. In the middle of all the flounce and fluff, was the tall, thin, bean-pole frame of the poor humiliated Catherine.

Chapter 2 — *The Glam, Gorgeous and Ghastly*

For a moment I thought she must have hired it from a Rogers and Hammerstein wardrobe. Poor Catherine looked horribly embarrassed but I assured her she looked stunning and we managed to get a little grin for the photographs but it did indeed take an awful lot of coaxing.

*　*　*

Darren and Joanne came to me with the usual stars in their eyes and not much else between the ears. But they were such a likeable couple. 'We're having a *Star Wars*' theme,' announced Darren as he sat down on the other side of my desk, cap on back to front and fiddling with his earrings. 'No we're not,' reminded the voluptuous Joanne sticking out her ring-pierced tongue for me to view? 'I thought we'd decided on Medieval.' '*Star Wars* definitely,' announced Darren. 'Gotta be *Star Wars*.' I had hardly said a word when Joanne burst into loud sobs, 'but you told me I could come as a Medieval queen,' she spluttered. 'Look,' I said, 'it doesn't matter what you choose to come as, you have heaps of time to decide — now let's get on with the paperwork.' I didn't want to get involved in the choosing of *Star Wars* and Medieval fancy dress costumes.

Medieval won out. Darren and Joanne advised me just before the wedding day that it was to be Medieval dress. 'And even our guests have been told to dress up or else,' said Joanne excitedly and she bounced up and down on a chair in my office. The guests turned up looking horribly embarrassed, wearing capes and with swords hung from their belts. They told me they felt foolish being asked to dress up and both mothers told me they cringed at the thought of it when they read their invitations. But they did not want to disappoint Darren and Joanne on their wedding day and reluctantly went along with it.

Darren stood through the ceremony, shoulders back and head held high — he had a bright yellow sun stitched to his chest. They had also chosen a long Celtic ceremony of candle lighting and paying respects to the elements, and while I, dressed in my long black velvet cape for the occasion, raised the elements to north, south, east and west, rang bells and lit candles, the guests cooked in the hot sun in their long, flowing hired robes. A few of them quietly disappeared into the bar during the ceremony as it dragged on in the outdoors heat. It was the exit aisle music which stole the show as swords and head-dresses started to disappear back down the aisle. Reaching over to the amplifier, Darren turned the volume control up as loudly as the amplifier would permit — Monty Python's 'Always Look on the Bright Side of Life' was a sure winner.

Darren and Joanne couldn't have been happier and I drove home to 'The Life of Brian' resounding in my ears.

＊＊

The lime green number was almost in the same league as the 'fucking red dress'. Lovely Irish Mary with her freckled face and red hair rather suited green but the shine was lime and there was no getting away from it. 'Green!' I heard guests exclaim as they spotted Mary walking towards us. 'Shit! Green!' exclaimed the groom loudly. 'It looks like slime on a bloody frog pond.' There's no knowing how a groom will react to his bride's frock on the Big Day. The tits are one thing — the frock another.

＊＊

One of the most creative numbers was a totally stunning, sequined, straight, black dress, with breasts to match especially for the occasion. The bride had sprayed herself with sparkly black and silver glitter, one of the most attractive brides I'd seen. She carried a classic, soft white bouquet, with four bridesmaids to match her colour and style exactly; the whole party looked absolutely brilliant.

But some sadly, wore totally hideous little numbers.

One bride turned up in her mother's pale blue wedding dress — 50s' style with little puffed sleeves. Her mother had wanted Carrie to wear something old and something blue. It was certainly old and certainly not new. It hung and sagged and so did the breasts. The frock twisted around her shoulders and the waist was lower on one side than the other, and the hem needed fixing. Such a shame because the bride was a lovely looking girl — but again, hadn't she heard of having a bra fitting to give herself a more uplifting and attractive look?

Over the years brides turned up at my office with their portfolios stuffed full of scraps of material and designs to show me, while the groom had to look the other way: strips of coloured ribbon and cut-outs of bouquets and buttonholes, a template for the perfect wedding or so they thought.

Some dresses were simply ludicrous, I could always tell when the bridal boutique had off-loaded a bad seller to some poor unsuspecting bride with the words, 'You look simply stunning darling; this is *just* the frock for you.'

Over and over, mothers of the bride and groom seemed to want to mirror the lovely bride and so made a grand effort to look like a bride themselves on The Big Day. Mutton dressed up as lamb was never a good look at the best of times, and many an old boiler would arrive with her skirt halfway up her thighs and breasts pushed up and over a ridiculous frilly little frock. A huge hat would make the whole outfit look like a giant golf umbrella. I called them 'brollies' which is exactly what some of them resembled.

It made a change when the fascinator fashion craze came in. This is when the mothers turned themselves into looking like Birds of Paradise plants instead.

But it wasn't always the brides who dressed to kill or alternatively, could have done better with their choice — sometimes the grooms took the prize for the unusual.

The Big Day

Richard and Emma were on a real budget Aussie tour and warned me they were not 'dressing up'. 'It's too hot Down-Under here in Oz,' said the groom fanning his pale, white English face, in my office after he'd arrived. 'You don't have to dress up,' I comforted them. 'It's your day and you can wear anything which makes you happy and that you feel comfortable in.' 'Would you mind if I wore a pair of shorts?' ask the groom a bit hesitantly. 'Of course you can — just come as you wish.' Richard's shorts were just that, short. Very short and very, very tight. Had he washed them and had they shrunk? And Emma wore a sundress as big as a square of tissue paper. But never have two people been happier posing in front of the Opera House for their photo shoot, breasts and all. I noticed the photographer's and his assistant's eyes never left Richard's shorts — not for a moment.

* * *

Funafuti is a town on the Island of Tuvalu which lies about a few hundred kilometres north of Fiji a small island steeped in tradition, so there were no surprises when shy Talikimuli arrived for the wedding wrapped in bright pink ribbons tied round his neck which flowed down to his waist. It resembled a pink lei and the bright pink ribbons fluttered left and right as the breeze blew across the harbour. He was from island nobility and these were the traditional colours and dress he must wear on the day of his marriage when standing proudly beside his lovely New Zealand Pakeha bride. They married at Copes Lookout in Kirribilli, once again with Sydney Harbour and the Opera House as a splendid backdrop for their romantic day.

This was one of the sweetest couples I ever had the pleasure of marrying, royal pink flowing Tuvalu ribbons and all.

* * *

Seamus too, was an absolute sweetie, and insisted he and his bride get married under a Frangipani tree which they found blooming near the Domain. He wore the most amazing long sleeved shirt — white with bright red, patterned strawberries. The shirt matched his endearing personality and after the ceremony, Seamus and his lovely bride took off to the pub to sample some Irish Guinness, before they slid off into the sunset to enjoy their marital bliss.

* * *

Garry was gorgeous too and about to make his bride a happy wife. He was immaculately dressed as were his groomsmen, but did he really have to turn up wearing joggers with his suit? The number of times even at the best of weddings where the groom wore joggers with a suit, was astounding, and I have also had short, little Asian brides sensibly wearing white joggers underneath their massive meringues, to give them height or to keep their feet warm and dry if they were having the ceremony on soggy wet grass in Winter.

* * *

One young Chinese couple who turned up with their parents to say 'I do', wore jeans and lucky red T-shirts with Chinese writing across the front which translated as 'Good Luck' and a sweet little thing called Jenny, had 'Weapons of Mass Distraction' emblazoned across the front of her fleshy Triple E's, while her jelly belly protruded between what was left of the shrunken bright pink shirt and the top of her ripped, hipster jeans. One groom proudly wore a T-shirt that said it all — 'Game Over'.

* * *

But never have I seen such happy couples as on their wedding day. Such were their individual dress codes: the 'Bold and the Beautiful' from the House of Forrester in all its elegance, the casual and tragic from Best and Less, to the bargain-hunted Vinnies' item. The Glebe and Balmain markets both produced quite a few vintage designer numbers which, from sound bargaining, ended up costing the brides less than the $100 on the swing tag. And I often felt the glamorous and beautiful boys of the Mardi Gras could have put many a bride to shame — roll on *Priscilla Queen of the Desert*, I often used to think and it would never have surprised me if Priscilla and her flowing pink number, had arrived for the ceremony, standing on the top of a bus.

※ ※ ※

Gay commitment ceremonies were often splendid affairs, where same-sex couples made their special promises to each other.

'Hi, this is Rachel,' was the throaty voice at the end of the phone. 'Do you do gay commitment ceremonies?' Commitment ceremonies were in a league all of their own. So it was no surprise then, when Rachel turned up on my doorstep, wearing a gorgeous metallic polka dot number and a voice equal to that of Pavarotti. Beside him stood Richard; they held hands smiling a little nervously, I thought.

'We've been together two years,' explained Rachel in his deep baritone voice, holding Richard's hand under the table. 'We want to make our own special commitment to each other.'

After much preparation and a ceremony written to touch the heart of the most toughened queen, The Big Day arrived. Their apartment was totally decked out with freshly cut flowers, the largest arum and tiger lilies I had ever seen. Aromatic vanilla and coconut candles and soft sensuous lighting completed the picture as the guests stood sipping champagne and dressed in some of the most exquisite numbers from the Oxford Street boutiques.

From pale pink cocktail frillies to crinkling tafetta and glittering beads, from the fluffiest of boas, the most outrageously huge fascinators, to the stalkiest of silver stilettos, the 60 male guests did not disappoint; it was to be a purely magical evening.

'Bloody eyelashes, darling,' I heard one bloke purr, 'they drive me simply silly.' 'Oh darling, fuck the lashes, just fuck me,' came a response from an aged, bronze beauty. Peals of laughter — then, 'Sweetie, for Godsakes, just *kiss* me; I'm starving but don't you dare smudge the lippy or I'll cry buckets.' 'Oh cry buckets, you stuffy old tart,' was the reply. 'Lippy's for taking off, darling, not for keeping on.'

'More champagne, dahhhlings?' called out someone in a sequinned slinky number, sashaying around the guests. 'Drink up my lovely ones; we're all here to celebrate, not to talk about fucking lashes and gloss.'

It was an absolutely beautiful ceremony, with Rachel and Richard crying the whole way through — black mascara streaking down both their cheeks.

There wasn't a dry eye in the house, and I detected a small lump in my throat which, for me, was most unusual indeed.

* * *

At another colourful commitment, the wig maker must have long since retired on the profits from The Big Day. From 60s' stark white/blonde bouffants to spiky millennium styles, they paraded before me. Not a hair out of place.

'Sweetie,' crooned a huge muscly-armed bloke in a gold glittery number, 'I'm damned if *this* really *does* do me justice.'

Patting his beautiful headpiece and rolling his eyes up towards the ornately corniced ceiling, he continued to address me: 'Wendy, if you've *ever* got to wear one of *these*, darling, then just *don't*; they are simply *too* horrid for words. I feel like a shagging Sherpa with a sheepskin on my head.'

'Brucey, just stop it darling,' came a voice over my right shoulder. 'You look simply divine. Anyway darling, I just love shagging Sherpas; just name the moment.' '*You* would be so lucky,' snapped the muscly-armed one, dropping a very limp wrist, hitching up the gold glittery number, 'I'd rather shag a sheep on my hands and knees, than shag you!'

'Girls and boys, this is too much on Chris and Jo's Big Day,' came the voice again calling through the noise of the crowd. 'Just forget the shagging for a moment, and let's get on with the ceremony. I'm just *dying* for a stiff one.'

At this point I wasn't sure whether a stiff one referred to a double martini with olives, a cocktail with a little pink paper umbrella or something else, so I just smiled and got on with the ceremony which again had everyone crying buckets and black, waterproof mascara making road maps down their cheeks. I'm still convinced though, there's no such thing as waterproof mascara.

* * *

'Light the bloody candle, darling,' whispered 68-year-old Jeremy, as 73-year-old Harry with his hands shaking, tried to light the match. 'It won't light, dear,' he whispered back, 'it just won't light.' Jeremy and Harry had decided to light a commitment candle during their ceremony; up until this time everything had gone smoothly — this was the first hitch. 'Harry, just light the bloody candle, I tell you,' urged Jeremy but the matches were damp and no-one had a lighter. Harry had been lucky enough to find an old box of matches in the back of the pantry cupboard just before the ceremony and hadn't thought to check if they would actually light. 'None of us smoke,' apologised Jeremy looking up at me. Harry kept striking the matches one after the other but none refused to light up. 'Oh stuff the silly bloody candle then,' said Harry getting even more impatient, 'I didn't want to have one in the first place.' 'Oh *yes* you did,' reprimanded Jeremy, looking up angrily. 'It was *you* who said we'll light a commitment candle.' 'I did *not*,' reminded Harry waving a rather limp wrist. '*You* told *me* quite clearly dear, a candle was to be the order of the day.' Frustration mounting, Jeremy leaned forward and grabbed the unlit candle off the table, and with one mighty thrust, flung it right out the open window down onto the street below. 'Right!' he said dusting his hands down the side of his frock. '*That's* what I think of *that* idea; now let's get on with the ceremony.'

Loud applause and cheering followed and even Harry managed a smile, and with both wrists dropped for effect and eyes again rolling towards the chandeliers, he finished by saying, '*Such* temperament, sweetheart, *such* temperament — how on *earth* did I fall into the hands of *such* a temperamental old tart?' 'Well,' concluded poor old Jeremy, 'what do you expect dear, from a raging old queen like you?'

* * *

Helen and Hope decided to wear matching outfits for their commitment ceremony and arrived, looking lovely and both wearing Indian salwah kameez. They had eyes only for each other and had supported each other through many years of family unhappiness and ill-health.

They were both very emotional during the lovely ceremony but it was a sad event, in that only five of the invited 40 guests turned up for the ceremony, and 40 places had been set inside the reception room; no expense had been spared. 'You are blessed today,' I told them. 'You have five lovely people here to support you; these five people are your true friends.'

The five guests rushed forward to congratulate Helen and Hope as I declared them 'partners for life'. Again there wasn't a dry eye in the house. I produced a box of tissues from my briefcase and we all stood with our arms around each other sharing the emotion of the moment.

They say you can count your true friends on one hand and this was certainly one of those times.

* * *

But it was the boys who mostly provided me with the most perfect, risqué entertainment.

'*Wax* darling!' spluttered a glamorous guest turning towards the 'groom'. 'My God — you have toooo,' someone else called out. 'You've waxed darling; just look at that smooth sexy chest — even your nipples stand out.' The groom beamed and unbuttoned his shirt for us all to see his smooth splendour. 'Smooth as a baby's bottom, my darlings,' he explained. 'I never thought I'd do it but I did!'

Apparently Simon had sworn on his tenth strawberry cocktail in Mischa's Bar one night, he would simply *never* wax but to please his 'bride' he had suffered the painful process and arrived home totally waxed from top to toe — the most perfect Brazilian despite the rash. The 'bride' Gerald excitedly demonstrated his approval by delightedly rubbing his hands over Simon's hairless chest, announcing, 'Is *this* how it feels, oh my God, I can hardly wait!' Waxing became the topic of conversation while we waited for the 'bride' to ready himself for the ceremony — most had a story to tell on the topic.

'Janet, the ol' queen actually *waxed* her pussy,' offered one of them, wrists drooping. 'She waxed it in the shape of a *heart*; I saw it and lethal it looked too, with her big pointy arrow jutting out through the middle of it.'

'Gorgeous — a waxed heart — oh, what a queen!' breathed someone in silver sequins, eyes rolling to the heavens and fanning his face with a white lace hanky, 'just what I fancy, a Queen of Hearts!'

A huge amount of shrieks followed and I too, totally doubled over with laughter, hardly being able to keep a straight face for the ceremony, but I managed to compose myself just in time.

Chapter 2 — *The Glam, Gorgeous and Ghastly*

The guests dripped and poured, and fanned themselves in the Summer's heat as the ceremony dragged on but just as I had finished, I heard someone say, 'Breasts and chests are usually so much cooler when they've been waxed, not to mention where it counts *most*.'

'Oh, just give me a Queen of Hearts, darling,' whispered someone in orange organza. 'I'll show him what a pierced arrow through a waxed heart looks like.'

I immediately thought of the nine pointy peaks of the Opera House and envisaged a pot of boiling wax slithering down its sides. Amazing how the mind works even without even one champagne under the belt.

Oh dear, it must have been the heat again. Damn these hot Sydney days.

* * *

Such were the wonderful commitment ceremonies I had the pleasure to perform; a welcome change from staring at the white meringues that didn't behave in the glare of the Summer's sun.

Chapter 3
Aspirations

'Come in Bully,' the famous lady herself greeted me at the door of her office. 'We'll get you sorted out.'

Dawn Fraser stood beaming as I approached; she was after all, our Local Member of Balmain where I was living at the time.

She had supported my previous application to become a Justice of the Peace and later as a Marriage Celebrant. But little did I realise the long wait to become a Celebrant. After repeated phone calls I was told by the Federal Attorney General's office, 'Nothing we can do to hurry all this up. You must wait for someone to move away or die in your area and then you can be appointed. You are just like a Post Office — only one in each area.' Having been heavily involved in the local community, mainly with the Balmain/Rozelle Chamber of Commerce, and as a speaker to groups such as Rotary and Probus, and after 30 years of Sales and Marketing the application form looked pretty good. But was I destined to become a Post Office? 'Good luck Bully,' the famous lady said with a broad grin, as I left. 'See ya.' I waited five long years until someone had died or moved away from the Balmain area, before I could identify myself as a Post Office.

* * *

The Big Day

With the sexy, the bawdy and the beautiful — the profession hung like a pendulum before me — but nothing had prepared me for the actual first knock on my door.

Envisaging a young couple, I was confronted by a silvery haired 73-year-old lady and her 72-year-old frame-leaning fiancé.

'Come in,' I welcomed them wide-eyed, hoping my amazement didn't show, too much. 'Lovely to meet you both.' The elderly couple were an absolute delight. They had lived together for twenty years and both had their respective children and grand-children, so *this* was to be my first official engagement. After a restless night I awoke to a raging head cold, blocked nose and a raw sore throat. Dosed up on Panadol I headed over to Ashfield to a lovely old Federation home meticulously cared for, both families already quietly assembled and waiting. But you could have cut the air with a knife — no-one spoke, they just stood and stared so I introduced myself and then with the bride and groom giving me the go-ahead, I commenced the ceremony but not exactly amidst the warm, happy wedding environment as I had expected. A couple of weeks later I called the couple to wish them well and hear all about their special day and was told, 'Wendy, it ended so terribly. We didn't tell you this before but you see, our families dislike each other intensely and they think we're both marrying for money and don't want to divide the family assets when we're gone. It ended in the most disgusting brawl on the front lawn and we had to call the police. 'Inheritances, dear,' she went on, 'can be such awful things; it was simply just too dreadful. All they want you to do is die,' she continued, 'but I don't plan on doing that for a while yet.' During my time as a celebrant, the number of weddings where families would not unite when the bride and groom were of mature age and obviously of substantial means presented a very sad state of affairs indeed. Inheritances certainly got in the way of happily married bliss.

* * *

Funerals fell into the same category and the dearly departed were not always loved or even liked, by their family. In fact many loathed the sight of the dearly departed and with the deceased body lying under the quilt in the next room, many were delighted and greatly relieved that this was the reason they were actually all under the same roof. Sitting at the dining table writing a deceased person's eulogy amidst the family's tears of sorrow or gladness, I would often encounter the bold and the ugly.

* * *

With emotions running high, sons and daughters, brothers and sisters, aunts and uncles, so-called friends and foes would speak not so lovingly of their dearly departed to the point of almost trashing the house and leaving with armfuls of family belongings such as chinaware, paintings, furniture, family memorabilia and so on. One family member manoeuvred the lounge suite out onto a trailer waiting in the drive as I discussed the ceremony, while amazed relatives just sat and stared. A daughter who 'hated the dirty old creep' wrenched a painting off the wall, gave me a withering smile and with the departing words, 'Got to run to the hairdressers,' left without a glance to the remaining family members but turned up at the funeral with her hair beautifully styled, dabbing the corners of her eyes with a neatly pressed handkerchief. Some grief!

* * *

At another pre-funeral meeting, a son of the deceased arrived as I sat speaking with the bereaved wife and her other children. Not wasting a minute for any type of formalities, he grabbed his dead father's car keys off the kitchen bench and headed off out the door, declaring, 'Got the bastard and got the beast — he owed it to me.'

Talk about death rearing its ugly head.

* * *

'Marge was just an old bitch,' announced another — the only sister and living relative of the dearly departed at another meeting. 'She deserves to be dead, serves her right. She made my life an absolute misery with her flashy ways and showing off about all the money she had. Just write what you like Wendy,' she said getting up about to leave, 'I'll show you out, see you at the funeral, and for heaven's sake, I couldn't give a damn what you write, but throw in the Lord's Prayer for good measure, and while you're about it, Psalm 23 is another one we may as well have. Won't do her any good though now she's gone. I inherit what's left of the money anyway, well ...' she finished, stopping suddenly in her tracks and glaring down at the three snarling cats at the bottom of the steps. Then looking up at me with a horrified look on her face she concluded, '... not unless she left it to the RSPCA!' I was often left wondering how the settlement of estates were finalised and whether there was even more gnashing of teeth when relatives discovered there was nothing for them to inherit apart from an old cracked teapot, a cupboard full of mothball-saturated, smelly old clothes and a stack of unpaid bills.

* * *

Mrs Lambert was a dear old soul and made a nice hot pot of tea on my arrival, and brought out some freshly baked scones. 'Here you are luv,' she said. 'Get some of these into you — my old Bob loved a fresh scone for morning tea.'

The scones were certainly delicious and the cup of tea well-made.

I settled back to discuss the funeral ceremony but Mrs Lambert was in no hurry to talk funeral ceremonies; instead she

Chapter 3 — *Aspirations*

launched into the family history and pointing to the mantelpiece said, 'Look luv, see those seven urns?

Well the one on the far left is my mum's ashes. God bless Mum, such a lovely old lady — now scones were her favourite too. Of course in the war years when they had to have coupons to buy the flour, well …' and on she went as I nodded and smiled empathetically.

After devouring her second scone, Mrs Lambert continued. 'Now the second urn on the left is my dear old dad, Arthur his name was. Very close we were. Well, he got killed when his tractor skidded into a ditch and it fell over on top of him. Also a scone lover and loved Mum's scones!'

Mrs Lambert devoured her third scone. 'Now the next urn — that large one there, well that's my cousin Richard. He had no family after his wife died, so he came to live with us. Talk about a sense of humour, a great bloke and fought in both wars. Used to be a builder but hurt his back and never really got over the death of his wife — that was Claire, you know,' Mrs Lambert informed me, looking up from her fourth scone.

'In the middle there is my sister Margaret,' continued Mrs Lambert pointing to the next urn. 'Didn't like her much; we never got on. When Dad got killed on the farm, she wanted to bury him because he was a Catholic but I said she wasn't allowed to make that decision. Anyway I didn't want Dad rotting all that way down under the grass. I wanted him up on the mantelpiece with all the others. Anyway, it's much warmer up there over the fire. I can assure you Wendy, I wasn't too popular at the time but I never liked Margaret — spoilt little kid she was, always getting her own way.

'Now on the right of Margaret,' Mrs Lambert went on, 'well that's my other sister Lizzie — we were twins. Identical. Folk couldn't tell us apart except Mother always dressed her in pink and me in blue. I miss her most of all I think; couldn't bear the thought of her ashes being scattered in some rose garden or other, so left her on the mantelpiece with all the others. Warmer there. She deserves to be up there with the others. Got breast cancer and that was the end of her; snuffed her out real quick, it did.'

Mrs Lambert gave a huge sigh and reached for the last scone, and then without hesitation, moved on to the next urn. 'Now the two small urns on the far right — well one's James. He was my youngest brother and the next one is Harold. He's the middle brother. Good brothers and they both stayed on the farm until it got too much for them. Never married, neither of them; looked on me like their mum once she passed away. Anyway, I couldn't scatter them either. I like to talk to them every time I'm dusting,' she continued looking up at me. 'I tell them they're much better off where they are instead of out there shearing and droving. Hard life out back, and anyway, it's warmer on the mantelpiece when the fire's going,' finished Mrs Lambert picking the crumbs of her plate.

'And now, there's only me left,' Mrs Lambert stated wistfully looking down at her empty scone plate. 'Bob and I never could have children, so what do you think I should do with all these urns, before I die too?' she asked. The next hour became a debate as to the pros and cons of burial or scattering of ashes.

'Just call me at any time,' I told her, 'once you've decided what to do with them, I'll help you along whatever path you choose regarding the urns.' As predicted, I never heard from Mrs Lambert after her dear husband's funeral and I now suspect there are eight urns on the mantelpiece to dust when Mrs Lambert does the dusting and eight urns keeping warm when the fire's going on a cold Winter's night.

* * *

'But we've got to have doves,' declared one tearful daughter. 'Mum would have wanted that.'

Chapter 3 — *Aspirations*

'How about doing it as the coffin is lowered?' I suggested.

'Sounds good to me,' sobbed Rose. On the day of the funeral, as the coffin was lowered under a clear, blue Australian sky, the cage of the six white doves ('Mum's lucky number') was opened.

But these doves weren't in any hurry to leave and no amount of coaxing was going to make them flap out of their cage.

Shaking the cage and banging on its side made the poor doves even more anxious but finally they hopped outside onto the lawn and then flapped nervously skywards but not before one decided to poo from the heavens above, down the front of the pall bearers black suit jacket. 'Lucky omen,' I whispered to the pall bearer.

'Yeah right — should have brought my bloody shot gun,' he answered back. Driving away from the cemetery, I envisaged a lone, black-dressed, pall bearer taking aim with a .303 and knocking six white doves out of the sky, white feathers gently floating down towards terra firma.

* * *

Slowly but slowly, wedding and funeral bookings trickled in, and I went about my duties in the expected manner but nothing ever prepares you for the totally unexpected.

* * *

Brimming with confidence, off to wedding number five I went — a gorgeous couple were marrying on a rocky ledge at the top of Shelly Beach at Manly, overlooking the beautiful blue Tasman Sea. Pulling up in the car park, I noticed a large police rescue van. Three boys in blue in full safety regalia were securing themselves with ropes and gently lowering themselves down over the side of the cliff face.

The Big Day

Putting my head out of the window I asked what they were doing. 'Just practising,' came the standard reply. 'Routine procedure,'

That statement always amused me, as did, 'We are just eliminating you from our enquiries.' Shades of 'The Bill', I always thought. I settled myself back into my car seat to await the arrival of the groom and guests; however, it wasn't long before the police officers were scrambling back over the top of the cliff edge, hauling a heavy green body bag behind them. Fearing the worst I called out again. 'What on earth's inside that bag, a body?'

'Yes, lady,' came the reply, 'what does it look like?'

'Well, get the rotten thing out of here quickly,' I yelled jumping out of the car. 'I have a bride and groom about to arrive for their wedding and I don't want this sort of thing to spoil their day.'

'Can't,' replied a boy in blue. 'Got to call a hearse; the van's carked it.' Grabbing my mobile phone, I dialled White Ladies. 'Quick send a hearse,' I yelled. 'There's a body that's got to go to the morgue!' Response is generally quick when it relates to death and to their credit, the White Ladies arrived in record time just as the stretch limo with the bridal party arrived, cruising to a standstill in the car park. I learned to be very protective towards the bride and groom and to try and diffuse anything which might spoil their Big Day, dead bodies or no dead bodies.

* * *

Not being overly superstitious, I took a mental note that I was about to perform wedding number thirteen but thought no more about it. The happy occasion was scheduled for 8pm in a little back street night club, in Surry Hills, and as was typical of the area, a ramshackle building tucked away near an old but thankfully, disused dunny lane.

Chapter 3 — *Aspirations*

This was to be a Celtic feast-style affair. Long tables groaned with legs of chicken and lamb, loaves of bread, large bowls of fruit and vegetables and cheap casks of cardboard cantata. This was all to be consumed to the music from a little happy band of minstrels.

The stage where the ceremony was to occur was a rickety structure but it fitted the ten of us well enough. After I declared the happy couple 'husband and wife', Leanne and her groom grabbed each other and took one mighty leap over the traditional Celtic broomstick much to their guests' delight. But as the couple landed on the other side of the broom amid cheering and clapping, the whole stage structure suddenly collapsed and with our feet buckling beneath us we all tumbled into a huge heap to the sound of broken glass.

The platform, on which we had been standing, had been propped up with empty beer bottles and with our combined weight it had simply taken its toll.

* * *

Unexpected disasters can strike at the best of times but nothing takes its toll more, than being forced outside in the heat of Sydney, in the dead of Summer. When Grandad sitting in the front row dressed in suit and tie, suddenly clutched his chest, I knew he was in trouble.

His face was ashen white and the look of sheer terror in his eyes.

Guests screamed as poor old Grandad fell forward; the bride yelled for someone to get an ambulance and it was a time I didn't hesitate to use my CPR skills.

Thankfully Grandad lived on to tell the tale.

Luckily these sorts of dramas were few and far between but it taught me to always be as prepared as I could ever be, like a good old Post Office always ready to serve its customers, or the

The Big Day

ever-ready prepared boy-scout, for the unusual, unpredictable and unexpected on The Big Day.

*　*　*

When I became a 'Post Office', appointment was made by the Federal Attorney General but since the flood gates opened, every man and his dog can become a celebrant. Now one just sits a course and bingo! I suspect conflict of interest now exists in many areas, from function managers to wedding cake bakers performing the nuptials. Even my local dry cleaner is a celebrant. 'I clean their bloody dresses,' he told me, 'so I may as well see how they get them so bloody dirty!'

Often I am tapped on the shoulder by a dewy-eyed matron who says, 'What a lovely job and a great way to make some pocket money. I think I'll become a Celebrant like you,' and then, 'What've you got to do to become a Celebrant?'

If I hear those words again, I'll scream. My acknowledging smile ensures the person I'm friendly, so I explain 'I haven't got time to go through it all now as I'm off to do another ceremony, but I am happy to email you and provide all the details.' 'An email,' one hopeful old matron asked me. 'What's that?' So I sat down and concocted an honest letter which I sent to all inspiring old matron-type aspiring celebrants, enthusiastic pocket-money youngsters and enterprising uni students, cake makers and florists, wedding car drivers and invitation printers, wedding function organisers and photographers — they all suddenly came out of the woodwork. They all wanted to become a marriage celebrant and a lot of them did.

*　*　*

Having been tapped on the shoulder by the proverbial old matron or aspiring celebrant extraordinaire, stating they are the 'new breed of celebrant' who think you just turn up with a brief case and a big smile, started making me think about how to answer the expected celebrant question. Often though, it was a thump on my repaired and sensitive rotator cuffs from an old retired headmaster who I'd predict would crack dirty jokes, ad lib and turn up in a tired old headmaster's suit, with dandruff-covered shoulders who thought he'd make the ideal person to officiate at marriages in his retirement.

I therefore concocted the following letter to serve such a purpose:

Dear Edna

It was lovely meeting with you today and I trust the following is of assistance to you in making your decision about becoming a Civil Marriage Celebrant. Being a Marriage Celebrant is a highly professional and responsible profession. Celebrants are appointed by the Federal Attorney General. Appointed Celebrants are those who have generally been in business or who have held a professional role.

Remember, you are dealing with many legal situations and are responsible for each couple's legal paperwork and solemnising their marriage ceremony.

List of responsibilities:
As it is now a small business, <u>all costs</u> must be borne by the celebrant.

You will need to buy all the necessary legal stationery from the authorised Government printer in Canberra and also all your general office stationery from somewhere such as Officeworks, for example: Copy/Laser paper, DL white envelopes, boxes of white presentation folders, 500 business cards, 500 letterheads, 'With Comp.' Slips, folders, binders for bookings, computer, printer, photocopier, telephone, answering machine, fax, calculator, signing pens, general office equipment, staplers, cellotape, ruler, personalised stamps and so on.

- No celebrant can work without a mobile phone especially on the actual wedding days in case he or she is urgently required by the couple getting married.
- It is mandatory to have a locked office and you will also need to buy an office desk, guest chairs, lockup filing cabinets, book shelves and text books to create a comfortable and professional environment.
- It is also recommended that you are a merchant for Visa and/or MasterCard as not everyone deals with cash and few people have personal cheque accounts these days.

It is helpful to have a cheque account for any payments you make on behalf of couples or for refunds. These are organised through the bank and the costs are yours.

- A modern reliable car.

A public address system with amplifier and a signing lectern to carry on the day and a smart briefcase to hold your register and legal papers and personal items such as make-up, car key and purse are also absolutely necessary.

(A P.A. system is a must as the Attorney General's rules clearly state that all celebrants are obliged to have this so that the ceremony can be heard by all guests. My last system cost around $800 just to give you a guide. But a super model can be up to $2,500.)

A professional celebrant will also need to join a Celebrants' Association. There are several associations you can join such as the AMC or AFCC — there are fees associated with this. It is also advantageous to attend seminars and conferences. Each year all celebrants must also complete at their own expense, five hours' compulsory ongoing personal development. Insurances such as public liability, professional indemnity and personal accident are also essential.

Chapter 3 — *Aspirations*

- *If you start visiting clients and running all over the city and you break your ankle, then you have no come-back re claims. It is advisable not to visit clients because of personal safety and accident issues.*
- *If we default in any area, such as turning up late, we could get sued. Celebrants are now obliged to arrive no less than twenty minutes prior to the ceremony commencement (I believe it's best to make a habit of arriving at least half an hour prior) and we are obliged to wait for no more than twenty minutes if we have another commitment to attend.*
- *Everyone has a schedule to keep! Couples can't book you for the whole day.*
- *You also need your own Business Registration and an ABN Number — these need to be paid to the appropriate Government authorities.*
- *Celebrants also need to organise their own individual contractual arrangements with couples so that we all know our obligations and abide by them. This is also at your own expense.*
- *Advertising can be huge. These costs are enormous — mine have been in the vicinity of $10-12,000 a year. Internet set up costs, on-going website costs, yellow and pink pages, bridal magazines and bridal fairs are all areas of exposure so you must have clear marketing/advertising policies. Yellow Pages alone can be around $2,000 a year.*
- *You will also need to pay for a 'roadie' to assist you on your wedding days. He or she can carry the amplifier and the very heavy briefcase while you carry the lectern. If parking is a problem near the ceremony area which is often the case, you need your roadie to be able to drop you off at the venue and go and find a car park or parking station. Wearing a smart suit and heels in 35-40 degree Sydney humidity makes it difficult to manage alone. You could of course buy a roller bag or a trolley to wheel your equipment.*

- Parking costs mount up too, especially if you are parking in the city so all these costs need to be included in the couple's fee.
- The only free thing celebrants receive from the Government is a brochure to pass onto couples prior to marriage. This covers some basic family law advice such as marriage information, a few basic legal issues including name-change, taxation after marriage, the importance of making a will, health and welfare benefits and some legal obligations after marriage.
- If not computer-literate you will need to pay someone to type and print your ceremonies for the couples, and bind them accordingly.
- You also need to print your own marriage certificates for the couple, which you give them on the day of marriage. We must purchase the certificates ourselves from the Government.
- A reasonably stylish wardrobe (suits and shoes) must also be taken into account.
- The celebrant writes the individual wedding ceremonies after collaboration with the couples so you will need to allow time to meet with couples after the initial consultation.
- Public speaking skills must be excellent.
- Ability to speak with confidence to parents, family and friends.
- Business skills are necessary to run a successful business.
- One should be a well-known and respected member of the community and if you have time, be involved in your local Chamber of Commerce, Rotary, Community Charity Group or such-like.
- Being a Justice of the Peace is not a pre-requisite to being a Civil Marriage Celebrant but it is certainly useful for witnessing the mountains of documents that come across one's desk.

Chapter 3 — *Aspirations*

- *A mature outlook, assertiveness and confidence are important traits. Whilst we are not Marriage Counsellors we are often taken into a couple's confidence about a range of personal issues.*
- *Ability to answer any basic family law queries and basic immigration issues which may arise.*
- *Your communication skills must be excellent as frequent liaison with function organisers, photographers and occasional contact with the couple's family is necessary.*

Hours:

- *The day commences at 8.30am for telephone calls and e-mails.*
- *To cater for working couples, my appointment times are from 9am-9pm Monday to Friday and sometimes in weekends in between weddings.*
- *Couples usually require two appointments (paperwork/ decisions re ceremony).*
- *Time is required for the celebrant to write up the ceremonies, prepare the certificates, and other legal paperwork.*
- *Rehearsals take time.*
- *You must allow no less than two hours between each ceremony to allow for travelling, parking and set-up time. It must be taken into account exactly how far you need to travel in between each ceremony as to how many ceremonies you can fit in per day. No celebrant can survive doing only one wedding a day in the weekend taking into account all the costs involved.*
- *You need time to keep up-to-date with Attorney General Rulings.*

As I have pointed out, you must be totally committed to succeed as there are many established celebrants such as myself who are highly sought after. The field is very competitive.

> *It is not possible to have a personal social life as it is a hard, fully time-consuming task even though immensely satisfying.*
>
> *I trust this information assists with your decision about becoming a Civil Marriage Celebrant and I wish you every success if you decide to join the ranks.*
>
> *Kind regards*
> *Wendy Bull JP CMC*

* * *

It was just a hurried letter which I hoped didn't offend such a lovely person or the many other people who made enquiries over the years. I wasn't surprised when I received a lovely letter back from Edna:

> *Dear Wendy*
> *I really appreciate you taking the time to write and to point out what was necessary to become a celebrant. I have decided not to pursue this area of employment after all. There is so much more to it all than I thought. Again my thanks, and do please call around and have a cup of tea when you are next passing. My address is on the back of the envelope.*
> *Yours faithfully*
> *Edna*

* * *

Since then, about 90% of the people who have tapped me on the shoulder and asked me about becoming a celebrant, have been sent this letter — and I have never seen their names on lists of newly-appointed celebrants. I believe I have done a service in giving them true, realistic and relevant information, useful for their decision making.

* * *

Chapter 3 — *Aspirations*

Most annoying are the couples who'd call and ask: 'How much do you charge for a wedding?'

I am quick to tell them to get all their quotes in writing and to see exactly what the fee covers. Some unethical celebrants have been known to send a bill after the ceremony with their little list of 'add-ons'.

I remind them too, that the cheapest celebrant isn't the best. It is obvious that a celebrant who charges cheaply only provides a basic service, whereas a full-time professional is a much better option for a trouble-free day. Of course there are added on extras such as water taxis when officiating on the harbour or travelling to a harbour island, bank credit card charges, city hotel parking and so on … how could this all be explained on the phone? So many hours are spent emailing couples information so they are aware of what costs are involved. Meeting couples after work especially after a long hard day doing weddings and paperwork, can be tiring, so I invented the code L.U.D.

This simply meant 'Look Up and Down' so a notation in my diary of an L.U.D. simply meant a couple was coming to look me up and down, and waste a lot of my precious time while they asked impertinent questions such as 'What makes you think you're the celebrant for us?' and 'How do you rate yourself compared to other professional celebrants?'

I sometimes reminded them that doctors and lawyers don't get asked those questions prior to a consultation. What on earth did they think I was going to do — live with them in their grotty old rented flat full of unwashed dishes for the rest of their lives and wash and iron their clothes?

I wasn't being interviewed for a job for heaven's sakes; what did they think I was — an out of work drop-kick? With most of the couples who came to get married, I was old enough to be their mother and to be sat down on my own premises and asked why I should be the celebrant for them, made me want to laugh out loud it amused me so much.

Instead I generally just answered with a smile and said, 'You've been here talking to me for over half an hour, you've checked out my Ceremony Guide and you are aware of the costs involved and what they cover and you've checked on my website and credentials — I am sure this is enough information on which you can base your decision.'

'Are you pretty?' asked a voice on the end of the phone. 'My sister's celebrant was sooo ugly.'

I wasn't sure how to reply to that one so I just said, 'Come and visit me and then you can decide for yourself.'

Once a very picky upstart of a groom asked, 'Can you show me some testimonials?'

'Sure,' I said, 'there are seven books of testimonials right there in front of you.' But do you ask a doctor for testimonials before he examines you?

The couple flicked and read, and shared their comments but they didn't ask me to be their celebrant and I didn't want to be.

Surely one's website, a half hour visit and testimonials should be enough.

So many were time wasters and asked for appointments at 8.30pm or later so they could go home and have dinner *before* coming to see me.

But what about *my* dinner and *my* life, I felt like asking. I tried to avoid seeing couples during weekends, simply because half of them found something better to do or arrived late after stopping off at a garage sale or an open-house, and just wanted to waste my time.

Weekend Wasters or Tyre Kickers — as a colleague of mine called them — often didn't even bother turning up, never mind a call to say they weren't coming. But if they did call it was usually the same excuse. 'We're caught up in traffic,' would be the standard lie. The after-work sense of urgency was a better method of meeting couples, anytime between 5.30 and 9pm — after that they arrived tired or alcoholic, you could smell they'd

Chapter 3 — *Aspirations*

been to the pub before coming to see you or they reeked of smoke having shared a joint or two out in the car, before meeting the person who was about to marry them. The photographer and venue seemed to be the first things they would book and many times they would phone to tell me, 'We've forgotten to find a celebrant'.

How on earth did they think they were going to get married? More often than not, the celebrant was the last person to get booked and when there were no professionals available for the most popular 3pm-5pm Saturday and Sunday time slots. 'But we want you; you were my sister's celebrant — what'll we do?' they'd wail on the phone.

Sadly it was their problem: I used to reassure myself that if they were old enough to get married surely the celebrant and the venue would be the first things they should think about?

Oh no! It's the photographer to whom they'd pay thousands, who is going to provide those all-important lasting memories — certainly not the legal piece of paper, except when it came to divorce and then, it'd be the first thing they'd hunt out! Then they would probably start wailing again when the marriage certificate couldn't be found.

I recall only looking at my wedding photos about five or six times in twenty odd years and I often wonder just how many couples get entrenched in their wedding photos in the years after their marriage, on a Saturday night.

* * *

'You need passport?' enquired Tjin. 'What you need passport for?'

'ID,' I explained, 'identification. If you were born outside Australia you must show me your overseas passport or birth certificate.'

'I'm on Tourist Visa,' he replied, 'I don't know why you want to see passport.'

51

'Well,' I went on, 'I can't get you married to May without seeing it. How did you come into Australia if you haven't got a passport?' I asked taking a wild guess that he didn't possess one. Tjin looked down at the table, deep in thought. Then, looking up at me, he said, 'That's OK Wendy. I find another way to stay in the country.'

As Tjin headed for the door, I decided he wasn't really wanting marriage but May was a good idea and a safe option, and he thought by marrying her he would obtain automatic Australian permanent residency.

This is certainly not the case but it was a good attempt to try and stay in the Lucky Country. But where was his passport?

* * *

Yes, it's fun being a 'Post Office'. Strange requests and the interrogation process never failed to amuse and how I loved showing the 'up-themselves' and the 'only-ones-to-ever-get-married' to the door.

Didn't they realise the ceremony of marriage had been around since the beginning of time?

I often wonder if half of them are still cohabitating in marital bliss. Doubt it.

Unfortunately, only 53% of marriages go the long distance! The afternoon soapie 'The Bold and the Beautiful' once had a character called Darla (who thankfully got run over by her drunken sister-in-law and written out of the script).

Darla was all tits, bum and dumb, so I ended up calling those who were truly dumb and stupid a 'Dumb Dumb Darla'. I encountered many Dumb Dumb Darlas over time and Annabelle was no exception.

Dear Wendy (she wrote in an email from the UK),
Thought I'd let you know, I have just got a new email address.
Love from Annabelle.

Chapter 3 — *Aspirations*

But which Annabelle from the UK? I had three Annabelles from the UK on my books at the time. So I had to go right through my files and try and find which Annabelle had emailed me.

Or better still:

Dear Wendy
Ron and I have just moved to a new address, so please send the receipt for our deposit to our new one.
Love Jan.

No date of marriage or new address was on this otherwise blank piece of paper. Many times I'd receive a payment by mail — a Post Office Money Order was all I'd find in an envelope — but whose payment was it, amongst my hundreds of bookings? No date of marriage on the back or accompanying note. I also put a stop to direct bank deposits because of the same reason — I'd look at my bank statement and find amounts credited to my account but with no advice as to where they came from either so had to wait until someone told me they paid me months prior whilst all the time I was oblivious of the payment.

* * *

Daniella was another Dumb Dumb Darla, as dumb as they come.

'Wendy,' she asked me, 'what do we do on the day if it rains?'

'You and Joe have to work out a wet weather venue and let me know what it is,' I told her.

'What's a wet weather venue?' she asked.

Helloooooo?

* * *

'If it's raining,' Judith informed me, 'we definitely still want the wedding outside under umbrellas.'

The Big Day

'We can't sign the legal paperwork in the rain,' I replied.
'What legal paperwork?' asked Judith.
Hey, is this a legal wedding or what?

* * *

When Matt and Cino were visiting one night after work and going through the usual motions of completing paperwork, I asked, 'And what's your occupation, Matt?'

'I don't know,' replied Matt. 'What on earth do I put?' he asked looking up at me.

'I have no idea,' I said looking up at him. 'What *do* you do?'

'All sorts of things really,' replied Matt.

I eventually worked out he was in IT and had a variety of job responsibilities, so he decided on the words 'IT Professional' as he told me, 'Only a professional person could handle all the things I have to do.'

Some professional! He didn't even know what he did.

* * *

One couple informed me they were 'Super Executives'.

'And what *is* a Super Executive?' I asked them.

'Don't you know anything?' sniped Ms Nose-in-the-Air.

So I wrote down 'Super Executive' in the boxes which asked for 'Usual Occupation' and left it at that.

It bucketed down on their wedding day. Karma made a lot of sense.

* * *

It was surprising how many Dumb Dumb Darlas didn't know their mother's maiden names and when asked to complete the form themselves, didn't understand what the words 'Mother Maiden Name in Full' meant.

'What does "Maiden Name" mean and what does "In Full" mean?' they'd ask. They'd get on their mobiles during an interview to ask their parents what their middle names were. 'Dad, have you got a middle name?' asked Kenneth, another Dumb Dumb Darla.

'Bloody hell,' exclaimed Kenneth after he'd switched off the phone call. 'Wha'dya know? Dad's got two middle names. His whole name is Bob Charles Ken Chapman.'

I then had to ask if Bob was short for Robert and whether Ken was short for Kenneth, so I had to get them to call back to check, and invariably it was.

* * *

When a couple's Birth Certificates were eventually produced I'd always check the names off against them just to make sure their names were spelt correctly, and sometimes even these were wrong, as the parents didn't realise that what was on their child's Birth Certificate had either been entered incorrectly at Births Deaths and Marriages, or even more amazingly, they'd forgotten they had given their child a third name.

Sometimes I encountered names scratched or whited out on Birth Certificates and other names written in because they didn't like the names they had been given, so had just gone ahead and changed them by pen.

'What's your occupation?' I asked a groom-to-be, as I filled out the paperwork.

'Done lots of things really,' he replied. 'Been a painter, sparkie, truck driver and a brickie but you'd better write down that I'm a butcher — left high school after a couple of years. I'm not the sharpest knife in the drawer, you know.'

I was highly amused but he was certainly one of the loveliest blokes I have ever had the pleasure of marrying.

* * *

Phoebe left with a list of documentation I needed her to bring on her next visit to me.

I wrote on her list:

> 'Please bring to you next appointment on 5th May at 8.15pm the following ...'

A week later the phone went.

'It's Phoebe here, Wendy. You know the list you left me, well when do we come back and see you?'

'What's the date on the note, Phoebe?' I asked.

'Fifth of May,' she answered. 'Is that when we come back?'

'Yes,' I answered, grabbing my glass of red from my office desk.

'Wendy,' she went on, 'you know the list you left us, of the things to bring; do we have to bring all that too?'

It's no wonder a celebrant needs the occasional nightcap.

* * *

I often wonder what we used to do before the convenience of emails — well, 'convenient' if the recipient answered you promptly or knew what the answers were.

> *Dear Joanne*
> *I trust your wedding plans are coming along well, and I just wanted to know where you are staying in Sydney in case I need you urgently upon your arrival from London.*
> *Please give me the name of the hotel and the address/phone number if possible.*

Chapter 3 — *Aspirations*

> *Look forward to your reply.*
> *Kind regards*
> *Wendy.*

The reply came back three days later:

> *Dear Wendy*
> *We're staying in the big hotel right in the middle of the city.*
> *The travel agent said this is the one everyone stays in.*
> *We'll get a taxi there.*
> *Not long to go now, and we're getting very excited about our trip to Australia.*
> *Love Joanne.*

Wake-up Joanne, Sydney's an international city with about five million people in it and there are hundreds and hundreds of hotels in Sydney's CBD … wake-up Joanne.

* * *

And yet another:

> *Dear Wendy*
> *Have you got trains in Sydney because we don't like travelling on overcrowded buses?*
> *If you've got trains, then where do they go?*
> *Look forward to your reply.*
> *Regards Kelly.*

I replied:

The Big Day

> Dear Kelly
> Thanks for your email and looking forward to meeting you both.
>   Yes, we have a huge train system in Sydney and I have attached ten train timetables just to give you an idea of our city and metropolitan network. There are heaps more but I am not sure where your destinations might be so perhaps best to check out the following website etc. …

* * *

And yet another:

> Dear Wendy
> Dougie and I want privacy and don't want anyone to see our wedding. Will there be any tourists walking around the Royal Botanic Gardens on the day of our wedding?

Helloooo? Is this a tourist city or what?

* * *

And another:

> Dear Wendy
> My partner and I are coming to Sydney to get married.
>   We want to get married on June 15th next year because this is my birthday.
>   Please tell me your availability and whether it will be raining on 15th June.

So what am I now, a weather bureau as well as a Post Office?

* * *

Chapter 3 — *Aspirations*

Dear Wendy
The testimonials on your website are great and we'd like to come and see you but please tell me, are free obligation-free visits, free?

* * *

Another:

Dear Wendy
Can you please help me? I am looking for a celebrant for 8th August but I want one who will let me write my own vowels.
 Vowels are a very special part of the ceremony and my fiancé said he wants his vowels to be as personable as possible.

So many brides called them 'vowels' instead of vows. Hadn't they learnt 'A E I O U' at school?
 And many wrote that they wanted 'personable' vows, instead of 'personal'.

* * *

And another:

Hi Wendy
Are you pretty? Because we don't want an ugly Marriage Celebrant. My brother had the worst celebrant imaginable. She wore a jumper around her neck and a pair of jeans.
Josh.

* * *

And yet another:

Dear Wendy
We found your website on the internet and would love you to marry us as we have decided to elope to Sydney.
   Please can you tell me how many people live in Sydney as it's to be an intimate affair?
   Yours Marion

I couldn't resist the following reply:

Dear Marion
Thank you very much for your marriage enquiry and I am delighted to be able to assist you getting married here in Sydney — congratulations to you both.
   Sydney has approximately five million people but I am sure we can find a lovely private place in a little park somewhere.

* * *

And then to something 'down-under' which really cracked me up.

Dear Wendy
I don't know how to ask this but do kangaroos really hop down George Street in Sydney? We went to a show in London recently and there was this comic guy from Australia who told us they live in people's backyards and also hop down the street when the sun goes down but we don't like the thought of this very much as someone told us they had strong and dangerous back legs, especially when they jump up and kick you.
   We arrive on 18th.
   Yours
   Vera

So I wrote back to Vera saying:

Hi Vera

Thanks for your email and I am happy to answer your query.

No, kangaroos only live out in the bush and only come out at dusk to forage for food. I think the comic you saw must have been a very convincing person and I feel gets top marks for his presentation.

* * *

And yet another classic:

Dear Wendy

We arrive in Sydney on 23rd December but we are getting a connecting flight the same afternoon out to Alice Springs.

To save us coming to your place, please can you meet us at the airport to finalise the paperwork and please can you marry us in the arrival lounge so we can arrive in Alice Springs married? Can we meet you near the check-in counter and do it there?

Well, I did just that.

* * *

Another about Sydney:

Dear Wendy

Please can you tell me where Sydney Harbour is? Is it under the Harbour Bridge? Is it near the Opera House or is that a lake I see in the photo you sent?

* * *

And about the Royal Botanic Gardens:

> Dear Ms Wendy Bull
> We think we'll get married in the Royal Botanic Gardens. Are there flowers and trees there, or just paths?

* * *

And about getting married in my apartment:

> Dear Wendy
> We think we'll take you up on your offer of getting married in your apartment in Chatswood. We have 105 guests. Do you think we'll all fit in?
>   And if so, is it OK if we bring some Eskies and BYO for a few drinks afterwards?

* * *

This one wanted an appointment:

> Hi Wendy
> We're coming to Sydney to get married. I am meeting up with eight celebrants at 4pm in a coffee shop at Darling Harbour.

My reply:

> Hi Charlotte
> Thanks for your email, I'd love to meet up with you to discuss marriage plans; however, I only meet couples privately in my office and do not generally meet couples in coffee shops and certainly not at the same time as other eight celebrants would be there.

Charlotte's reply:

Chapter 3 — *Aspirations*

> *Hi Wendy*
> *There is no way I am going to go to your office. Lots of celebrants are happy to meet up with us at Darling Harbour so we can look them over. I know you are probably busy so perhaps you should take Business Management lessons so you can learn to organise yourself properly.*

I ignored the reply. What — travel all the way to Darling Harbour to a coffee shop? Incur travelling and parking costs? Spend two hours of my time just so they could look me up and down and line me up with eight other marriage celebrants? Do a bride and groom ever ask their doctor to meet them in a coffee shop with eight other doctors just to see whose diagnosis they agree with best? What a joke and how absolutely rude, especially as I have taught Small Business Management and Time Management for many years and have officiated at thousands of weddings! I pitied the poor celebrant they chose.

* * *

This Dumb Dumb Darla took the cake:

> *Dear Wendy*
> *Is this your real name? My sister's name is Wendi so I thought it was spelt Wendi? Are you sure you spell it with a 'y' at the end? Wendi Deng is married to Rupert Murdoch and hers is spelt with an 'i'.*
> *You see, my girlfriend at school was called Wendie, so I suppose there's a difference.*
> *Anyway, we want to get married on 30th December in Sydney. We currently live in Yorkshire — is Sydney very much like Yorkshire?*
> *By the way, we're from the UK.*
> *Please can you send me some info?*

> *Regards*
> *Sheilah*

Hang on Sheilah — think I know how to spell my own name. I've had it for ages.

* * *

Voicemail messages were often hurried and often if couples were calling from a poor reception area, I couldn't reply to them simply because I couldn't hear what they wanted and anyway, most forgot to leave their telephone number. I recall that I came home from a busy day of weddings and sat down to listen to all the calls which had come in, during my absence. 'Hello, I'm calling from England,' came a voice. 'We want to get married next year in Sydney please. Can you call me back?' No name, no number — Dumb Dumb Darla has a lot to answer for.

When answering the phone or an email, the most asked question to a celebrant is:

'Can you tell me how much it is to get married?'

I feel like replying: 'Of course I can. I'm the celebrant, aren't I? Why don't you just ask me how much I charge?'

Many couples don't understand that a 'Post Office' can vary its fees — different products, different services and different prices, and can vary these according to individual requirements and services provided?

'Is it the same price for a short wedding ceremony and only a few guests?' was another query.

'Yes, Melodie, because I still have all the same costs. I still have all the same paperwork, insurance, OPD, stationery, appointment, travelling and times costs. Just a short ten minute ceremony and only having a couple of guests on the day makes no difference at all.'

'But what if we just want the legal parts?' asks Melodie. Enough said.

*　*　*

Often couples arrived to their final appointment with only half the things needed for the paperwork, prior to marriage. It didn't matter how many lists I made them, there was always something missing, with the excuse, 'I didn't think you'd actually want this'.

Then, why on earth would I write it down?

The reality was that they'd forgotten to bother getting the info so the warning would come: 'No money, no honey and that simply means no documents and final payment — no marriage.' That always reaped the desired effect.

It didn't matter how often I told couples to always write the date of the wedding in the subject box of their emails, so I could find their booking in the month they were to marry, it was often not done. Instead I'd open up my emails to be confronted by a variety of subjects. The most popular title was 'Our Wedding' but with no date.

One such email read:

Dear Wendy
We've decided on the 'Apache Wedding Prayer' to be read at our wedding in June, so will you please put this in. And can you read it for us please?
Thanks

But who sent the email and what was the wedding date?

Did she really think she was the only bride getting married in June in Sydney? And did she think she was the only client, I had? The movie 'Dumb and Dumber' so often came to mind.

*　*　*

But the 'Apache Wedding Prayer' verse always made me freeze and was a huge favourite and often requested as a reading. Often couples would ask me, rather than a friend, to read this verse and because I've read it so many hundreds of times, I would be laughing inwardly, just managing to keep a straight face in front of my roadie and photographer. It was painful trying not to laugh out loud.

I eventually told couples I seriously couldn't read it for them so would ask them to find someone with good reading skills instead. 'But none of our friends are Australian,' wailed Minh. 'You very lovely speaking voice and nice smile; you read it, please Wendy.' The photographer and my roadie would grin broadly as I launched into yet another reading of the damned thing, so thrashed to death by every knowledgeable and good-standing celebrant in Australia. It was as much as I could do to contain my laughter. I must have said it a thousand times or more, and for those celebrants and learned people who know the verse off by heart, my tongue-in-cheek version, with apologies (I think) to the writer, goes as follows:

Wendy's (Tongue in cheek) Version of *The Apache Wedding Prayer*:

Now you will feel no pain
Because you've just got married,
For each of you will be eternally pissed
And far too pissed to care.
Now you will feel no more cold
Because the ravages of alcohol will not be missed
And your liver will eventually be damaged
Far beyond repair.
Now there will be no more loneliness
As your bottle and you are now one.
Because your vision has become blurred
And you're lying on the pub floor

Chapter 3 — *Aspirations*

*And when the barmaid smiles, you'll simply just ask for more.
You are probably two bodies because when your eyes stop focussing
Your vision becomes blurred and everything doubles.
But there is one life before you and one home,
And one damned good local drinking hole
Which will generally be
A writhing and slithering mass of bloody idiots
Not going home for tea.
When evening falls and you're on your back in Pub heaven
You'll look up and there she will be —
Through your bleary alcoholic gaze, a big breasty barmaid
Will be peering down
To see if you have passed out or died, maybe
And then you'll take each other's hand
(either your wife's if she's still with you but preferably the barmaid's)
And turn together to look at the road
You travelled to reach this ...
The hour of your happiness.
Together in total drunken oblivion to numb the reality of marriage
And as the future lies ahead,
You'll discover true happiness which
Is generally falling asleep at the bar over a couple of bottles of red,
a triple scotch,
a glass of neat gin,
a trio of martinis,
ten schooners,
a couple of midis of 100% proof rum
And eight for the road.
Your life will become a long and winding road
Between your place and the pub,*

Whose every turn means …
Discovery (of new labels on the market)
Old hopes (about beating alcoholism)
New laughter (because when you're pissed you can't help yourself)
And shared tears (of the remorseful alcoholic variety).
May the sun bring you new energy by day
When you've partially recovered from the depths of hell,
And may the hangovers disappear as quickly as they come,
May the moon softly restore you (with Vitamin Bs) by night,
May the rain wash away your worries
Of mortgages and a frigid, tired wife because the barmaid has much bigger tits and so much more to offer,
And may the wind blow new strength into your being
(that's if you can get it up and remember how to use it).
And all the days of your life
May the local pub always employ attractive, blonde and breasty barmaids
For the need to always see and feel their beauty
And may you keep drinking and live in a haze of alcoholic stupor
And tell the world to go get fucked especially the day before your wedding.
For your marital adventure … has just begun.

Again, enough said.

* * *

Amazingly though, despite coping with all the Dumb Dumb Darlas and their phone calls and emails I must have done something right and it was always gratifying to receive thank you cards and emails which have filled many boxes and ring-binder books over the years. Flowers have arrived from florists and slices of fruit cake have been delivered to have with our coffee.

Boxes of chocolates are a firm favourite as well as English Breakfast Tea, shortbread biscuits and mugs.

A book on cricket and a recipe book on how to bake bread once arrived on my doorstep.

A couple from the UK sent me a book on the TV serial 'The Bill' with a 'Bill' coffee mug and 'Bill' apron to match. Oranges and apples have also arrived, together with a very prickly pineapple which I donated to my brass Buddha in the hallway, as an offering.

In my mail box I once found a Chinese silk dressing gown and a tube of mascara. And one morning when I reached in for the mail, I discovered a lipstick and an offer for a health massage. I have also received some other lovely gifts — a beautiful tissue box cover from Thailand and a leopard-patterned scarf. I generally have no idea who has sent the gifts as, like emails, there no names given. One evening a young Thai bride-to-be arrived for her appointment with six plastic buckets of Thai take-away. She told me it would save my cooking dinner after she left. Another time, a couple presented me with a beautiful, coconut-scented candle. I must say the bottles of wine were always very welcome gifts, especially after a hard day in the office under the Southern Cross.

Chapter 4
An Attack of the Vapours

The heat on a hot Sydney summer's day can be deadly. And clearly heat and animal poo just don't go together. 'Mind the elephant poo,' called the groom as we all made our way to the bottom of Taronga Park Zoo. 'Step in it and you'll know all about it.'

'Bloody bastard,' I heard someone mutter. 'Thanks for the warning, mate.'

Trying to get rid of poo off your shoes is an almost impossible task, and if you actually manage to, the smell still sticks around forever. Parks located in Birchgrove and Balmain were the worst for doggy poo although I encountered a retirement village once in the Southern Highlands which allowed its inhabitants to have their pet dogs live with them. I had just commenced a lovely ceremony for a mature-aged couple when a little white yapping dog raced around the corner of a block of apartments with its very elderly master in hot pursuit, waving his walking stick. The terrified little creature made straight for the groom and bound up against his trousers, yapping as it looked around. It then turned and darted across to the father of the bride and lifted its leg most ungraciously against him, and peed as only a little dog could pee after being chased in hot pursuit, right down the side of his trouser pants. 'Whiskers, Whiskers, come here,' croaked the old man struggling across the lawn waving his stick, but little yapping Whiskers just went racing around and around in circles sniffing the grass and then, selecting a nice spot right in

The Big Day

front of the bridal party, it unceremoniously crouched and did a poo of which only little Whiskers could be proud.

Its elderly owner arrived on the scene full of apologies but little Whiskers had already done its damage much to the horror of the bride and groom.

* * *

But the poo incidences kept popping up and sometimes I thought my career should have been in marketing for the World International Toilet Expo., perhaps selling a Rust Buster or a Super Sucker, and after sixteen years, like breasts and booze, poos and loos, this would also be an interesting facet of my daily work.

One morning setting up for a wedding in the Illoura Reserve in Balmain East, I kindly asked a lady walking her dog to remove her dog's poo, which it had left behind, before she moved on.

'I'm about to perform a wedding here,' I explained trying to smile as kindly as I could.

In true yuppie 'would-be-if-she-could-be' style, Ms Designer-Tracksuit, with her nose stuck up in the air and the dog dragging her along, turned to me and the guests, and loudly told us all to, 'Go get fucked.'

A thinking celebrant will be prepared for all situations and I learned to carry rubber gloves and a plastic bag — not that I would clean up any animal poos but at least I could save one of the groomsmen from getting his hands dirty. The gloves were good too for gathering up syringes, tissues, fancy-pants underwear (lost in the dark and in the passion of the moment), empty pizza boxes, beer and wine bottles.

Now since local councils do not adequately provide garbage bins because it costs them too much to collect and return, you can bet that any park will have its fair share of doggy poo and garbage the morning after the night before. You name it; parks

Chapter 4 — *An Attack of the Vapours*

have it. Certain councils should be ashamed of themselves. On many occasions I have had a baby who clearly needed a nappy change thrust into my arms and if there's something that isn't kind to the nose it's poo. For this reason I have never held a baby at a Baby Naming ceremony and as much as I dearly love children and babies, I have learnt to leave the sometimes smelly privilege to the parents.

But anyone would understand why I almost had an attack of the vapours when a bridal couple told me to stop the ceremony halfway through, to haul their screaming baby out of its stroller.

Thrusting the baby into poor Grandma's arms the bride said, 'Quick change James, Grandma; you can smell him from here.'

Grandma laid little James down on the lawn in front of me and bridal party while the bride threw Grandma the baby bag, and with poor old Grandma down on her knees in her best Mother-of-the-Bride outfit, she proceeded to change screaming James in full view of everyone including poor Martin the photographer who was starting to turn a whiter shade of pale.

Baby James, pleased to be getting some dry nappies on and with the cold air hitting his naked front, decided a pee was in order of the day and like the Tivoli Fountain, shot forth hitting poor Grandma in the face.

* * *

I can guarantee that at any wedding where there are babies and young children, there will be interruptions and noise, screaming and yelling.

The string of strollers get lined up like cars in a car yard down Parramatta Road. They are packed sky high with toys and bottles, diapers and dummies.

Surely couples could find a sitter just for a few hours for their friends' wedding but no, they want to show off 'the child' as it is generally referred to, to anyone who is remotely interested in its screaming open mouth and smelly bum. 'The child' doesn't need to be subjected to a juvenile jail on a 38 degree day and secured in a safety harness just to make matters worse.

* * *

On another memorable occasion I had the loveliest bride who was eight months pregnant with twins. It was another typical Sydney scorcher, her almighty bulge stuck out in front of her like a front end loader.

'I've really grown,' she sighed, 'even in the past few days since I've seen you Wendy. Come on; let's get this over and done with as I can hardly stand.' Natalie's feet were as swollen as rising dough, as she struggled up the aisle, the back of her dress held together with safety pins, and the guests offering a spontaneous round of applause and cheered as she approached me.

The poor groom, I could see was suffering along with his bride and he clutched hold of her when she reached the altar. 'Oh to hell with it, Wendy,' she groaned, 'just do the legal parts and let me get out of here.' I launched into the Monitum and vows and it was as much as poor Natalie could do to finish repeating her promises but we got there ... I declared them 'husband and wife' and after a quick kiss, Natalie struggled as fast as she could to the door. 'What about the ring?' called the best man holding the ring box up in the air. 'Oh forget that,' answered the bride's mother grabbing them and shoving them into her handbag, 'her fingers are far too swollen. Anyway the hospital will make her take them off when she goes into theatre.' But poor Natalie couldn't reach the door, she sunk into the first available chair, legs wide apart and head thrown back just as the first pain sharply hit.

'They're coming,' screeched poor Natalie. 'Quick, call an ambulance.'

'No time for that,' yelled the groom. 'Someone get a car.'

Chapter 4 — *An Attack of the Vapours*

Each of Natalie's painful contractions produced a piercing scream, and between four guests and the groom, they eventually manoeuvred poor Natalie into the back seat of one of the groomsmen's cars. I called the next morning to learn Natalie had produced identical twin boys much to her hard-earned relief — after she'd emptied the scotch from the best man's hip flask during the drive to the hospital.

* * *

But a wedding wouldn't be a wedding (according to many) without a cute little winged fairy flower girl or two. But cute little flower girls have a habit of getting very tired, and very, very quickly. After a morning of fuss and hairdos, and putting on frocks, ballet shoes and wings and being told to 'stay out of trouble', by the time the cute little flower girl reaches the wedding ceremony, she has become very niggly and cross. More often than not, the guests' attention is just on the flower girls because they look so lovely and sometimes the bride is forgotten in the whole spectacle of The Big Day. Everyone stares at this little miniature ballerina while the poor bride and groom try and make the best of getting some attention. One absolutely scorching Summer afternoon in the Royal Botanic Gardens, the bridal party consisted of two little flower girls, three-year-old twins, Chloe and Zoe.

Chloe and Zoe were dressed in pretty pink tulle with fairy wings strapped to their backs. As the ceremony dragged on, Chloe and Zoe lost interest and the little pink ballet shoes became a target of their fascination as their little feet got hotter and hotter. Suddenly Zoe plonked herself down on the grass as the ceremony was in full swing and loudly announced, 'Bugger these shoes, Mummy,' and proceeded to rip them off with Chloe following suit, giggling and tugging at the ribbons around their ankles.

The Big Day

'Stop it,' hissed their mother, who was Matron of Honour. 'Leave them on.'

'No, I won't,' cried one of the little pink fairies and promptly lay on her back with her legs parted, wide in the air facing the guests. 'I'm hot Mummy; take my shoes off Mummy.' Chloe thought this was wonderful and copied her sister by also falling onto the grass, and both giggled furiously with their legs wide apart, up in the air, much to the amusement of the guests and to the delight of the photographer. Reaching up to her feet, with her little legs still pointing towards the heavens, with one final tug, Chloe pulled her shoes off and quickly she gathered up both pairs of little pink pumps and made a dash for the duck pond, flinging them in, much to the surprise of the paddling ducks.

Zoe followed her sister running across to the pond, shrieking with delight at seeing the ducks, but not before both little girls had ripped off their panties and stuck them on their heads for effect.

Round and round they ran in their bare feet, fairy wings flapping behind them with their pants firmly stuck on the tops of their heads. How I kept a straight face I will never know. I always find it so amazing that little three year olds can run much faster than adults when in hot pursuit in wedding regalia. It must be something to do with the wings.

* * *

But children love weddings and the excitement is often just overwhelming and so forgetting about toilet procedures until desperation point occurs, it is not uncommon to hear, 'Mummy, I want to go to wee wees' in the middle of a ceremony or worse still, 'Mummy, I've just done poos in my pants.' I am always being asked where the toilets are, and it's something a good celebrant has a memory for at each location.

* * *

Chapter 4 — *An Attack of the Vapours*

It never ceases to amaze me the number of couples who were pressured into having their nieces and nephews and friends' children attend the wedding with loud hints of, 'Why don't you ask my Gemma if she'd like you to be a little flower girl?'

'But I don't want to have a flower girl,' the bride-to-be would offer.

'Go on,' the mother would urge, 'she's so cute and 'you'd love to be a little flower girl, wouldn't you, Holly?'

How does a bride get out of that one?

* * *

I recall a lovely bride whose two already married bridesmaids boycotted the wedding the day before The Big Day, even after the bride and groom had paid for their dresses, shoes, makeup, hair, underwear, flowers and gifts just because they wouldn't back down on what had been requested in the invitation that 'Only adults attend, please.'

Consequently, because the bride refused to change her mind after months of nagging, she was told most unceremoniously on the phone, she could 'go get fucked if the kids can't come.'

* * *

Visiting me one night was a couple who explained that they *had* to have their two nephews as pageboys to hold the rings. With warning bells ringing I gently suggested they weren't quite old enough to be responsible for holding the rings.

'Josh and Tyrone are gorgeous kids,' said the bride, 'they're three and four. They'll be fine with the rings, trust me.'

I'd given the warning and learnt not to interfere as after all, it was *their* Big Day, not mine. And so The Big Day arrived; a cold blustery southerly had blown up from the south and Sydney Harbour was peaked with white tips.

The Morpheus heaved up and down in Farm Cove, and Josh and Tyrone with it. The little lads looked lovely but this didn't match their patience during the ceremony, for suddenly I heard Tyrone announce, 'Go on, bet you can't throw yours as far as mine.'

The bride swung around and yelled, 'No! Don't you dare,' just as Josh raised his arm and the ring fell out of his hand and rolled towards the edge of the boat. The best man, a front row forward in size, immediately lunged forward performing a first-class tackle and saved the day before the rings rolled over the edge of the boat and hit the bottom of the harbour floor.

* * *

Gift giving often went a bit haywire, too. Thinking it was a good idea to give the little children of the bride and groom a gift during the wedding, after the bride and groom gave each other rings, sounded a wonderful idea. 'Brianna and Michaela,' I said, just as the vows were to be repeated in front of 120 guests, 'your parents are delighted to have you here beside them today to share this very special occasion in their lives — the day they marry. And now they have a lovely gift for you both.' There was dead silence from the crowd as they craned forward to see Brianna and Michaela accept their gifts. With their tiny outstretched hands, little Brianna and Michaela accepted their beautifully wrapped gifts and tearing off the pretty wrapping paper they both stood stock still and looked up at their parents.

'A bracelet?' queried a peeved Michaela. 'I don't want a silly bracelet; I want one of those new big space dolls we saw on TV.'

'And I don't want one either,' copied Brianna. 'I want one of those big space dolls too.' With that, Brianna and Michaela burst into tears and thrust their little gold bracelets back into their mother's hand.

'But you both always said you wanted a pretty gold bracelet,' she explained puzzled.

'No Mummy,' snapped Michaela. 'I want a space doll, not a silly old bracelet. Anyway, I need to do poos, so where's the toilet?'

It doesn't matter how many times you prepare couples to not give young children responsibility on their wedding day, they just can't resist having a pretty pink fairy or a little suited pageboy dressed to kill in a penguin suit. Sometimes gift giving isn't a good idea either. Looks of disappointment can often kill what should be a memorable wedding mood.

I call them FWDs — Fraught with Difficulties or should that be, Fraught with Disasters?

* * *

You couldn't beat some lovely country ceremonies with a romantically dressed-to-kill groom who had tied yellow ribbons to the trees just prior to the bride's arrival or one who laid dozens and dozens of whole red roses as a bridal carpet.

One dashing groom erected a sign along the road leading to a grand country homestead which read: 'Your Beauityful'.

Yes, some were truly romantic.

* * *

The middle-aged Sydney-slicker blow-ins, who were dressed to kill and typical of the new Southern Highlands property owners, would have bought the land cheap from a broke old farmer, erected a beautiful home and without any knowledge of farming or land and livestock management, commenced their alternative weekend lifestyle.

Therefore, as the ideal venue for their daughter's wedding, Mr and Mrs North-Shore went the whole hog with no expense

The Big Day

spared, from the white marquee to the five-piece orchestra, to the portable dance floor, caterers, truckloads of flowers and crates of chilled champagne. Sophie wanted to have her ceremony in an undulating paddock fairly close to the newly erected mansion under an immense gum tree, the perfect spot except Mr North-Shore himself, had no idea about cattle and thinking he was doing his daughter and guests a favour by keeping the grass as low as possible, he let his stock into the paddock the night before so that the grass would be nice and short for the memorable occasion the following day. But what goes in must come out and **80** Poll Hereford steers in a small paddock overnight do not make for such a great ceremony venue with mounds of freshly excreted poo and a zillion flies buzzing around in crazy delirium.

The smell was horrendous in the mid-Summer heat and the whole time poor Sophie and Nick, and everyone else, furiously brushed away the flies that landed on any exposed part of the body while guests skirted around the offending piles of poo.

The Australian Wave went full bore that day.

* * *

Animals can create some amusing and sometimes, hair-raising moments but I must admit, I'm not often told about one's pussy even on the day of the wedding. I was duly on the doorstep in good time prior to the scheduled 11 o'clock ceremony and stood ringing the doorbell ... but no answer.

I rang and rang and it was only after thumping once or twice that the door was opened by the small shy and retiring bride-to-be.

'Hello Wendy, do you like my pussy?' asked the little Thai lady who stood smiling at me. 'I got very nice pussy.'

Standing there in a fluffy white robe, I could hardly make out the pure white fluffy feline she held in her arms. 'My pussy very soft and fluffy,' she finished innocently, batting her eyelids.

Chapter 4 — *An Attack of the Vapours*

Whether it was a touch of sunstroke I'd got in the past few days of working out in the Summer heat or the fact that I wasn't prepared for this comment as I opened the door, I couldn't help roaring with laughter as I stepped inside. 'You can pat my pussy if you want to, Wendy,' Chantana finished. I was left holding the fluffy white cat for a whole hour, while she ran up the stairs to haul her husband-to-be out of bed to commence the bathroom process, and wondered just how a more serious celebrant would have reacted to this comment or whether they would in fact, have reacted at all. Let alone wait for an hour while the bride and groom showered and dressed for their all-important nuptials.

* * *

Unfortunately many a park or lookout point in a National Park does not offer toilet facilities, so one must 'make do' if one really has to. Beside most car parks in the bush and even on roadsides, you'll see mounds of white toilet paper people have left behind and I can guarantee that most trees near pull over areas are very well watered and manured. But Charmaine was fortunate, because there was a construction site right next to the ceremony area they had booked for their wedding.

'I'm desperate,' she confided in me as she struggled out of the bridal car. 'Must have been last night's curry. What on earth can I do?' Looking around I noticed a portaloo positioned inside the construction site but the first hurdle was getting over the two metre high fence into the yard.

With three bridesmaids who didn't give a damn about the bride wanting to have a poo, my roadie and I helped her over the fence, holding up metres of white organza so it wouldn't snag, but getting Charmaine into the portaloo was another story.

How on earth was she going to fit inside with the two of us holding up her larger than large hooped, wedding dress? With my roadie's eyes averted and holding up the front of the bridal gown, I squeezed inside with Charmaine and helped her down with her underwear, a mean feat with stockings, a suspender belt and a blue bridal garter to contend with.

Charmaine managed the all-important task of 'going' but there was no toilet paper, so we donated the handkerchiefs I had stuffed down my bra and lost them to the portaloo company for good and for all. But how some of those portaloos smell! I now even dread the look of them as there are simply too many reminders of desperate situations.

If I could have banked a dollar for every time I've had to contend with a poo situation or to help a bride pee, I'd be a very rich celebrant indeed.

* * *

After a whole day out on the road, it is often me who is the one in the desperate situation. So it's a welcome relief when I am shown where the loo is at someone's house and off I race down the hallway to the welcoming and delicate little sign which reads: 'Here 'tis.'

'It's down the passage on the left,' Ronald the groom pointed out, 'and the bathroom's next to it.'

'And Wendy,' he called as I was about to slam the door behind me, 'just a bit of a warning here, don't use the handtowel by the basin.'

'What's wrong?' I asked.

'Oh, Mum uses that instead of toilet paper; she's a pensioner and saves on the Sorbent,' came the apologetic reply. A good celebrant is always prepared, so out came the antiseptic impregnated towel wipes from my briefcase.

* * *

But nothing offends worse than BO and a dose of halitosis hitting me in the face. I was greeted with the sloppy, limp handshake of Bryan who was wearing a sloppy, lopsided toupee. 'Hi,' Bryan said, introducing himself and breathing right into my face. 'I'm a friend of the bride.'

Dave, the 'bride', glanced over towards us, 'Oh, hello Petals,' he crooned. 'Like the new toupee!'

Bryan rolled his eyes skywards and letting out a huge halitosis sigh which struck my nostrils like a whiff of Taronga Zoo, replied, 'Ooh, ooh, darling, **I** didn't think you'd notice.'

'Have you a partner here?' I asked halitosis Bryan trying to engage him in conversation.

'No, just said goodbye to him, we were together fifteen years.'

'Oh, I'm so sorry,' I replied.

'And just why should *you* be sorry?' asked halitosis Bryan breathing across my face again.

'Well, it's not always so happy parting from someone, especially after all that time together,' I offered.

'Huh,' snorted Bryan, the halitosis hitting me right in the face once more,' I was looking for something a lot more than just friendship.'

'And that was?' I enquired.

'Love!' screeched Bryan fanning his halitosis wildly towards me, 'I want a lover, someone to love!'

* * *

I can just see my sister Carol with her head thrown back, laughing out loud and fanning her hands in front of her nose as she often would, saying: 'Bring me the smelling salts dear, I'm having a sudden attack of the vapours'.

Chapter 5
Keeping up Appearances

Strange, the people who walked through my door. Especially the ones who knew everything. 'Such beautiful plants,' commented Ms Glance-at-Myself-in-the-Mirror, as she looked out onto my balcony, and as she flicked her long extensions followed by a glance into the mirror by my desk.

The main aim of flashing the huge sparkler on her wedding finger was obvious.

'Of course I'm a passionate botanist and know all my plants — thoroughly. I studied botany — topped my year, I have actually got many degrees, in fact they say I am over-degreed.'

With one more glance and flick of the extensions she rose carefully to her feet and squinting through her glasses, looked again out onto my balcony.

'Your Spathiphyllums are lovely, Peace Lilies of course, and what shiny leaves. You have looked after them well … and I'd say they are around six-nine months old?'

Without waiting for my reply, she continued.

'So,' she asked as she came back to my desk, glancing at herself in the mirror as she did so and flicking a stray piece of hair that had fallen over her right eye, 'what do you feed them?'

'Nothing much, well, nothing really,' I said. 'They'll probably live longer than all of us put together.'

Ms Glance-at-Myself-in-the-Mirror gave me a puzzled look but I kept on with my paperwork, while she kept glancing and flicking the long blonde extensions. One must keep up one's appearances for sure, and I didn't want to deflate Ms Glance-at-Myself-in-the-Mirror's ego — just yet.

Well, not until after I'd married her off; then I'd tell her the reason the Spathiphyllums would definitely last longer than all of us put together and never needed watering, was simply because they were only the plastic variety from Target and as I had informed her, would probably outlast us all. So much for the many university degrees and being able to recognise a plastic plant from a real one.

* * *

'Hi Steve,' Rick drawled in his Southern Californian accent, 'How're ya doin'?'

I introduced Rick and his bride to Steve the photographer who leaned up and shook hands.

Steve was on his knees rummaging through his camera bag.

'What ya lookin' for?' drawled Rick.

Without looking up, Steve said, 'Hi Rick, just getting another lens.'

I winked at Steve and said, 'He's a very conscientious bloke you know Rick; he actually only does this photography thing part-time. He's really an astronaut.' I quickly glanced across at Rick who I suddenly saw had an incredulous look on his face.

'Oh my Gard,' drawled Rick, 'an astronaut — really? Well I be dogonned; now just wait 'til I tell the folks back home we've met a real live astronaut — oh my Gard, and on my wedding day too.'

I didn't have the heart to tell Rick it was just my sense of humour that made me say what I did, for Rick had believed what I'd said and I didn't want to disappoint him.

Being within earshot, the bride came tripping over in her flouncy little cream coloured frock. 'Oh my Gard,' she also drawled, 'well fancy that, a real live astronaut. Let me shake

Chapter 5 — *Keeping up Appearances*

ya hand.' If there was anyone who didn't fit the image of an astronaut, it was Steve.

Photographer — yes, astronaut — a definite no.

Both of us found it hard to keep a straight face throughout the ceremony and I promised him, I'd never put him through that one again as they didn't let up the entire time he was with them during their photo shoot and even wished him well on future blast-offs as they left. My sense of humour never really let me down — a surviving celebrant needs one.

* * *

Then one day I had the most gorgeous couple from Ireland.

'This is Steve, the photographer,' I introduced. 'He's really only a butcher but don't tell anyone,' I concluded light-heartedly. 'Me dad's a butcher,' said Patrick looking most serious, 'God rest 'is soul. Ended 'is days 'e did; tripped and cracked 'is skull inside the cold room — found 'im cold 'n stiff as a board we did.'

Niamh, squinting her eyes in the glary Australian sunlight, eyed Steve closely. 'Well, you sure do look like a butcher, Steve; d'ya tek photos of farm animals, 'n' all?'

Steve shot me a look that'd kill a brown dog, so I left it at that and suggested we start the ceremony.

I think Patrick caught the twinkle in my eye.

* * *

Darlene made contact from deep in the heart of Texas as soon as Mr Drop-Dead-Gorgeous-and 35-years-younger-Chuck-the-Stud proposed; after all, why wouldn't he?

Darlene, who was as skinny as a piece of A4 and botoxed and face-lifted to the hilt, owned three cattle ranches. But having no computers on any of the ranches made contact difficult so

87

Darlene would phone every week to make sure I was on track with everything for her Big Day.

Darlene insisted on marrying on a boat so she and Chuck the Stud could sail around Sydney Harbour and marry in Mosman Bay, because this is where she had been born. Her mother was originally from Mosman, where her father, an American Naval Captain had fathered their beloved daughter and heir to the family fortune before they sailed to settle permanently in America, to make their fortune. Darlene wanted an Aussie feel to the wedding so during one of the phone calls she had requested small meat party pies, 'tomayto ketchup' and 'lots of vodka'.

'But you guys order anything you want — just do me proud with the pies and vodka,' she had drawled. Darlene had been able to rustle up three long lost Aussie cousins from Nimbin who arrived at Circular Quay indeed looking like long lost cousins; had never been to Sydney before but had been born in the hills of Nimbin, and who resembled three wild, pot smoking hippies from an old black and white American flick. Sailing into Mosman Bay, Darlene eyed the party pies and 'tomayto ketchup' but not before she had consumed three large straight vodkas in the hope, presumably of putting on some more weight. Her pink frock hung like an oversized potato sack around her skinny frame and Chuck the Stud was swaying with the Sydney Harbour tide underneath one of the largest Stetson hats I'd even seen. The three hippies from Nimbin clutched the railing of the boat with one hand and their pot with the other, while I legalised the union of Darlene and Chuck. 'Of course we insist you join us for dinner,' drawled Darlene over her fifth empty glass of vodka and tossing a hardly nibbled party pie into the harbour. High up over Sydney in Restaurant 41, in a private dining room we feasted on anything we wished, no expense spared but Darlene and Chuck, preferring their packets of Winfield Blue and the three hippies from Nimbin preferring their pot to potato au gratin, disappeared down into Hunter Street where they were able to smoke, while my roadie

Chapter 5 — *Keeping up Appearances*

Philip and I sat around the empty table for seven, wondering why we had been invited there in the first place.

So on our own, we feasted to our hearts' content. We ordered and ate, wined and dined, pampered by three eager waiters. Finally finishing and the group not having reappeared back up from Hunter Street, we went back down to street level, where we said farewell to poor skinny Darlene and the new Texan ranch owner, and the three straggly hippies from Nimbin, never to be seen or heard from again.

Steve was one of the photographers I had an enormous amount of fun with. I could trust him implicitly to be there on time and to get the photos processed without delay and he was a damned good photographer to boot.

But whilst I had an enormous amount of fun it certainly wasn't the same with all the photographers I met on my rounds as a celebrant. They certainly weren't all as positive and friendly as Steve. Some were plain difficult and I am sure they thought it was their day and not the brides. Setting their equipment up in front of the mums and dads so they could get the perfect shot of the bridal couple is not in my mind, the behaviour of a professional operator.

I experienced many a photographer standing plum in front of the mother of the bride so that she couldn't see a thing but instead she had to watch her beloved daughter marry the man she loved, while leaning around a photographer's backside. A horror husband and wife team showed up from time to time. They always delayed proceedings, asking me to go slowly while they leaned, stood, lay and climbed themselves around the bridal party. A small ladder was always positioned behind the bride and groom so that they could run up to the top of it at the time the couple exchanged rings as their camera lens zoomed in and out which was a particularly annoying habit.

* * *

But I always said to myself — the couple chose them, not me, so I would walk away knowing I had acted professionally at least. Photographers have a habit of delaying brides and bridesmaids getting to the wedding by firstly taking what seems like 45,000 shots as they were made-up and then of the bride with a rose between the teeth, draped across the bed in her bustier, followed by the wafer thin body of the bride climbing into the wedding meringue and squeezing the over-sized meringue into the bridal car. Then more photos again at the ceremony venue as the car arrived with the meringue trying in vain to get out through the car door. After succeeding, the photographers insisted on draping the meringue with the body inside over the bonnet of the Rolls (like the Kim Cantrell ad), around the door, through the window and any other position they decided upon. Breasts and cleavages, as usual, were always a priority and many a time I stood and watched a photographer insisting the bride lean this way or that to get that perfect shot.

They never seemed to have any consideration for the poor groomsmen, guests and celebrant standing around in the blazing hot sun waiting for the bride and her entourage to arrive.

'Would you like me to refer a photographer?' I asked the couple from the UK. 'Maybe just a small package to capture the special moments of your ceremony?'

'No thanks,' replied the bride-to-be on the phone. 'Our daughter has studied photography and will be coming with us to take the pics.'

Sadly, this comment became all too familiar. I have witnessed many stuff-ups of friends and family doing the all-important job of photography, and have been given many feedbacks of disastrous outcomes. Why don't couples value the skills of a professional photographer? Cheap isn't always best and many of them have learnt the hard way: either no pics of their Big Day, or a few hardly worth taking down to the local pub.

Chapter 5 — *Keeping up Appearances*

The daughter who had 'studied photography' arrived with her camera and prepared herself for taking the all-important pics of her mum, the bride and partner Cliff.

'Oh no!' I suddenly heard her say. 'My batteries are flat.'

'No Cheryl. Surely not,' wailed her mother. 'When did you last use your camera?'

'About two years ago,' Cheryl replied looking a bit sheepish.

'Wendy,' asked the bride, 'have you got any spare batteries?'

'No sorry,' I replied, 'and the closest shop is a fair way away.'

A look of thunder crossed Cliff's face as he hissed to his bride, 'I told you not to trust Cheryl with anything.' So I called Steve to see if he could come and save the day but he was already out on another job. Feeling sorry for the bride and groom, I took a few pics after the ceremony on my digital camera and sent them to the couple in a beautiful little flip photo album. Situations where a 'friend' did the photography invariably ended in disaster. One couple, trying to save money rather than hire the services of a professional photographer, asked their friend to take the wedding pics but the friend quickly became a foe after it was discovered that she had forgotten to put the chip back into the camera. Friends can become enemies very quickly when they fail to deliver.

Appearances, it's said, are pretty much everything and first impressions are supposed to count. But not always.

Know-All Norm fell into this category. I'd married off Know-All Norm quite a few years ago and it didn't surprise me when he turned up on my doorstep with Bride Number Two, informing me Wife Number One had post-natal depression after the birth of their first child and sadly they couldn't work things out, so they decided to call it a day and were divorced. Know-All Norm seemed pleased to see me again and introduced me to the new bride-to-be, a stunning 'girl of the night'. But nothing had changed. As likeable as he was, marriage hadn't improved his posture or his wobbly chin and smart-quip know-all comments.

The Big Day

He proceeded to tell me about all his bad business deals, losses and partner who'd ripped him off and embezzled the profits and left him with the debt-collectors hammering at his door.

Not his fault of course; nothing ever was. During our interview I asked him whether he'd like some referrals to photographers.

'Nup — mate of mine will be doing all this — free of course, one of Sydney's best; it's not what you know, it's who you know,' he informed me, his chin wobbling along as he spoke.

I knew better but just left it at that.

'I've also got a guitar bloke coming — I'm going to be his new promotions manager; he'll be famous by the time I've finished with him — world-wide … you know … I'll be flying high. Anyway wait 'til you hear him on the day, you'll be blown away.' Yeah right, I thought, so will the confetti and probably the novelty of marriage after a couple of days. The Big Day came, with Know-All Norm arriving and sucking on a can of bourbon and coke.

'Where is everyone?' I asked.

'Comin',' replied Norm. 'Dropped 'em off up the bottle shop — need some more of the good oil.'

He went on without me saying anything.

'Gunna get an upgrade tonight at the Shangri-La,' he started boasting. 'Know plenty of people, you know.'

'You'd be bloody lucky,' piped up a rough-neck mate who'd turned up and who was also sucking on a can of bourbon and coke. 'All the bookings are done on a central system thing.'

'I know the "Maître d"' — friend of mine,' answered Know-All Norm.

'Fuck mate,' replied Rough-Neck, 'the Maître d' can't upgrade you; how bloody stupid's that?'

'I'll do it,' replied Know-All Norm, chin wobbling and dripping with bourbon and coke. 'Know heaps of people around the place. Anyway if that doesn't work then we'll go down to Darling Harbour somewhere, closer to the casino; *she* wants to go there after the Chinese banquet.'

'Anyway Norm, where's the photographer you said was coming?' I asked deciding to change the subject.

'That's me,' replied Rough-Neck.

'And your camera?' I asked looking around for his camera bag.

'Doesn't work,' he told me.

'Jesus mate, what d'ya mean, ya camera doesn't work?' exploded Know-All Norm swinging around so that he spilt even more bourbon and coke down his floppy fat chin.

'Don't worry, I'll borrow one of the guest's digitals,' he concluded as he wandered off to the Eski to look for another can.

'And what about the guitar player?' I enquired.

'Can't come,' Rough-Neck called out from the Eski, as he cracked open another can. 'Can't come — just had a call.'

'What?' spluttered Know-All Norm, spilling what was left of the bourbon and coke down the front of his shirt. 'Can't come? I'll get the bastard for this.' A scruffy concoction of guests started to arrive, some a bit on the dodgy side of things, so I started the ceremony while the bride chattered away to the groom, and the guests chattered even louder to each other, even though I said, 'Shush shush,' a couple of times no-one seemed to bother about why they are really there. One guest answered her mobile and chatted away in Cantonese through the entire ceremony. Suddenly it was time for 'vows' and I asked the bride to repeat her vows after me. But the bride decided she didn't understand English after all, when asked to repeat her vows after me, so to attract attention from the chattering guests, she decided to hide behind her bouquet and smile coyly at Know-All Norm, asking loudly, 'What she say? What she say?' Then she decided to drop the ring on the grass and giggle loudly to attract attention, and after that started to fan her face in the heat with her bouquet.

Rough-Neck the photographer was nowhere to be seen. I presumed he'd gone for a leak behind the bushes and getting another can of bourbon and coke, but no-one was taking photos; they were all just talking in Cantonese.

It sounded like they were catching up on recent events at Sha Tin and Happy Valley racecourses. The wedding over and Know-All Norm looked up from signing the Marriage Register and asked: 'Where's Johnno gone?'

But no-one appeared to care less — let alone me, the last time I set eyes on Rough-Neck was when he was sucking on a can of bourbon and coke and probably wishing he hadn't been asked to the wedding in the first place.

* * *

I advised couples so many times not to get friends to take the wedding pics; it was always best to leave this to a professional person who knew what couples wanted. And to hire a photographer … who actually owned a camera that worked.

* * *

A nasty photographer many celebrants encountered, would delay the bride, I am sure out of spite. One day I met the bride's car as it arrived and the guests, having already waited 40 minutes after the appointed ceremony starting time, were withering in the heat.

I politely asked Ms Nasty-Photographer to hurry things along as the guests had already been waiting for some time only to receive an icy stare and a bitter remark telling me to 'kindly fuck off'. What came out of her mouth, I decided, would even make an artificial bridal bouquet wither. It always seemed to be the women photographers who displayed 'attitude'.

For some reason, the men were generally so much easier to liaise with.

With respect to many a photographer, I always cringed whenever I was aware that a woman photographer unknown to me would be turning up, because of the attitude that she would undoubtedly display.

'I'm Jake,' said a young sounding voice behind me.

Turning around I was confronted by 'Jake' the photographer, obviously a new one around the traps.

'Hi Jake, I'm Wendy the celebrant.'

'I'm the photographer,' he announced beaming. 'I've just done my TAFE course … my first wedding; come on then kid, let's give it a whirl!' he concluded.

'Give what a whirl?' I asked the young man who appeared to be about nineteen.

'The wedding, of course; come on let's show 'em how it's done.' I dreaded the outcome of the photos for the poor bride and groom but again, it's not my problem whom they choose to capture those precious moments on their day. Like the services of a celebrant, cheapest isn't always the best, I thought again. Jake literally danced around the bridal party snapping this and that, and posing the bride and groom in a 60s' style line-up.

I could see the parents of the couple were not impressed either by his continual banter of 'Come on, let's give it a whirl.' But Jake had other motives — either that or he was plain stupid for Jake started to become amorous — youthful charm at its worst. Hang on, I thought, I'm old enough to be your mother.

All through the ceremony Jake had been winking at me, with one eye on me while the other was behind the lens.

I couldn't get to my car quickly enough afterwards and hoped he wouldn't chase me across the gardens to ask me for my business card. And again, I often wondered how a photographer could wink with one eye and take shots with the other, and whether the happy couple were indeed happy with the finished product. Doubt it.

* * *

The Big Day

Whilst trusty Steve was prompt and reliable, others weren't. Another scorching day in the Royal Botanic Gardens, we waited in vain for the photographer to arrive. The groom and few guests who had all flown in from overseas, melted in the heat while the bride hid behind a clump of bushes waiting for the perfect entrance. But where was Gaz?

There was only an automated message on his voicemail when I called and I broke out in a nervous sweat expecting the worst.

I called continuously, leaving messages but no photographer appeared, so we had no option but to start without him. The worst scenario — no photographer.

Thankfully I had my trusty digital, so my roadie willingly took some shots which turned out quite well and I was happy to send them on to the couple after the wedding in a pretty little Aussie souvenir photo album.

Sadly the couple from overseas had gone to every trouble to make their day perfect. They had asked me to arrange for the red carpet, chairs and the floral bridal arch for them to stand beneath — the arch also framing the view of the Opera House and Sydney Harbour Bridge for those special shots. But the non-arrival of the photographer was absolutely devastating.

The next day Gaz called full of apologies — he'd forgotten to put the booking into his diary which I thought was a lame excuse for a professional photographer with a studio, so I quickly dropped his business cards into the recycle bin, took him off my website and thankfully, never encountered him again. No second chances, in my books, for so-called professionals who fail to appear.

* * *

The more photographers I met, the more I was convinced they were a similar breed to celebrants, although, one thing about photographers was that they never really displayed a sense of

Chapter 5 — *Keeping up Appearances*

humour, especially the women — but at the end of the day a sense of humour was paramount. If only they could have realised it. The wedding industry is full of horror stories but there again, no-one's perfect and you always have to find someone to blame. Horror stories abound and of course, it's never the bride and groom's fault. Never — how could they ever be wrong? After all, they get married every day of the week and know it all. Yeah, right.

* * *

Freda had already changed her appointment four times and the phone went. Freda, according to Tony, is attending TAFE today; therefore they can't make their appointment at 1pm.

'But today is a public holiday,' I tell Tony. 'How come she's at TAFE?'

Tony says he doesn't know; he'll call her again and find out.

Tony calls again and tells me, 'Yes, Freda's at TAFE.'

I swallow this one like a bucket of fish and make yet another appointment.

'Maybe we can't come to that one either,' Tony confesses, 'I will ring you tomorrow.'

I am picking Freda's gone to one of the Winter sales which have just started or she's found a new sideline squeeze somewhere else. Freda and Tony were scheduled to get married the following week and there were still legal documents to be sighted. I'd called continuously for the past six weeks.

If they're old enough to get married, I'd think to myself, then they are old enough to cop the responsibilities of marriage and all that it entails.

But does turning up to an appointment mean it's a responsibility? I am still convinced that couples think you sit and wait for them all day and that you have nothing else to do. Tuesday night and the phone went again. 'Wendy, we're running late; can we make it at 10.30pm and not 9pm as we haven't had tea yet?' And what about my tea, I think to myself. 'Sorry Tony, I go to bed at 10.30pm,' I say.

'Well, when can we come and see you then?' Tony is starting to sound put out.

'Tony, I get up at 5.30am to answer my overseas emails and start appointments at 8.30am and finish at 9pm. Can't you possibly make it anytime on Monday to Friday between those times?'

'We have soccer practice Monday nights, and Freda does TAFE Tuesday night, Wednesday night we go to her mother's place for tea and Thursday night we do our shopping and on Friday night we have drinks after work and then go out for dinner.' I give up on Freda and Tony — and tell them if they don't come before Friday night then I can't do the paperwork for their wedding and that means no wedding.

Tony rings back again and says they will come that same night at 9 o'clock because Freda is scared of not getting married because into the bargain, Freda's just become pregnant and if they don't get married, Freda's mother will kill both of them. Surely couples can see the importance of getting their legal paperwork completed and surely they know I can't see them on Saturday afternoon when there are weddings to perform.

* * *

'Wendy, can you come to our place instead of us coming to yours? Twirl my cat's sick and we can't make it over to Chatswood,' Christina whined on the other end of the phone.

'Christina you live in Liverpool and I live in Chatswood, I wouldn't have time to travel there and back because I've got other appointments booked.'

'I'll call the vet,' offers Christina, 'and see if he'll come and look after Twirl at my place, while we come to your place.'

Chapter 5 — *Keeping up Appearances*

Christina calls back.

'The vet said we can take old moggy to his place, and he'll put him down instead of just cat-sitting because he's fifteen and the vet said he's going to die soon anyway. See you in about an hour,' concluded the bride-to-be.

Poor Moggy. Twirl's time was up for sure.

* * *

Nothing is prettier than a beautifully decorated wedding cake; they were often the major centre piece of the reception room. And they generally cost four times as much as they paid the celebrant who paid for all the legal paperwork, typing and travelling, not to mention all the stationery which used to be free from the Government, but now wasn't and the insurances which were mandatory, and all the other things which mounted up on the spike.

Sharni's cake cost $1,800 and had been baked, iced and packed carefully by the makers, and driven to the resort on the back seat of the bride's mother's car, safely transported with the safety belt around the box so nothing could possibly happen to it except that Sharni's mother didn't know that wedding cakes with icing don't like sitting in hot boxes on the back seats of cars during mid-Summer.

Poor Chef couldn't help mouthing the F word when he opened the box to find the whole cake sunk in the middle and filled with a melted mass of white icing. He immediately instructed the bride's mother to be present in the kitchen as a witness, as he tried to lift the sunken cake with its melting mass from the box. 'I can't possibly repair this properly in time,' Chef stated turning to the distraught Mother of the Bride. 'I'll do my best but no promises.' As Chef started to lift the icing with his knife, it became apparent that this was no ordinary cake. The cake was in fact a round piece of thick

99

foam rubber, skilfully covered in marzipan which had been covered over with icing.

In the heat, the foam had simply absorbed the sweet sticky mess of marzipan and icing, and sunk to a hollow bearing the weight.

The Mother of the Bride was absolutely horrified, to think that someone had made the cake out of foam rubber and had iced over it and thought they could get away with it! Chef did his best to remodel the 'cake' but it was decided not to have the traditional 'cutting of the cake' after the main course. Instead they decided to tell the guests it was only for show and it would be distributed after the honeymoon.

But like other wedding horror stories there was a predictable ending: the bakers had *not* 'forgotten to bake the cake' in the cake shop, for the cake shop was no longer a cake shop on the couple's return from their honeymoon but a closed and boarded up premises and the occupants long since gone.

You can scam it up to Noosa on $1,800 and have a bloody good time on some wedding cake money.

* * *

First impressions are wonderful things and bless the bride who made my day by arriving in the most glorious, bright, tangerine coloured frock. The guests' cameras clicked continuously as she made her way along the red carpet.

Looking resplendent she had it all — brains, breasts and beauty, and a passion for all things colourful. Being a florist by trade she had arranged her own bouquet of gerberas in purples, oranges, reds and pinks. Another stunning bride — and a beautiful girl to go with it.

'Go and have a look at the table decorations,' she told me during the signing of the register. 'Tell me if you like what I've done.' So off I went afterwards to have a look. Perfect. Picture perfect. All the tables were adorned with tangerine coloured table napkins and tangerine coloured gerberas, and upon each table was a large brandy balloon with two live tangerine coloured goldfish inside each one — they matched the gerberas perfectly.

The whole setting was one of the most original and tasteful I had ever seen. I called the bride a couple of weeks later when I knew she'd be back from her honeymoon to ask how things went. She was quick to fill me in on all the minute details of the reception. 'Wendy, you wouldn't believe what a wonderful time we had, especially Glen, the best man,' she said. 'Well, by the time the speeches were over, he was totally pissed. Totally. He went off staggering around the tables, sculling the water from every brandy balloon, chewing and swallowing the goldfish as he went.'

I could barely listen to the whole story and heard later from the photographer that he had used his creative skills and had gone berserk with the camera, even rushing outside to capture the best man chundering up in the rose garden. 'No fish on the menu that night?' I couldn't help asking, and we both collapsed laughing at our respective ends of the phone.

A keen sense of humour is a prerequisite for both celebrants and especially photographers. It makes the day so much more interesting and, as in the 'Life of Brian', it's much better to look on the bright side of life. But being a flexible celebrant is also important; there is no such thing as 'an ordinary wedding'. 'Cats,' Marion told me, 'I just love cats … my Mopsy is coming to the wedding in his cat cage.'

'Your cat?' I asked. 'Yes, you'll love him, if you love cats. He's a bit of a moggy — you know, an ordinary fluffy black and white bitser type thing but I just have to have him there. I've even got a special poem I want read out. Here,' she said shoving it in my hand. 'Read it,' she demanded. Here is what Marion got me to read for her, on The Big Day.

The Big Day

Pussy
'He is only a pet' they think or say
passing on their way
through my empty day.
'He is only a pet,' they say, and yet ...
He shares my laughter and my tears
through all the memory laden years.
He sleeps beside my pillow white
Nudging me gently through the night.
Then purrs with his little wake-up call
Time to get up, one and all.
He's the love who curls in my lap.
How can anyone argue with that?
My pussy I love with all my heart
My hubby comes second, right from the start.

I suggested *The Owl and The Pussy Cat*, which at least made mention of marriage but Marion was hell bent on the *Pussy* verse, and so it was read to an amused audience.

And the connotation of the word 'pussy' in the last verse, wasn't missed by too many, I can assure you.

* * *

Denise and Edward's wedding was scheduled for Callan Park — so hopefully no hiccups and unwanted guests, just us and the witnesses and photographer. I was told they wanted something really laid back, and so laid back it was.

The bride and groom came ambling across the grass eating hamburgers, their dogs jumping up trying to get some handouts.

'That smells good,' I said as they approached. I'd been out on the road all day and hadn't eaten a thing. 'We're starving too,' said Edward. 'Here, we've got some fish and chips as well,' Denise offered munching on her burger and leaning inside her shopping

Chapter 5 — *Keeping up Appearances*

bag. 'We haven't eaten either; we're starving — here have some.' So taking up their offer and not wanting to ignore their hospitality we all sat down on a tartan rug spread out on the grass and ate every last piece of battered fish and greasy chip. So, I then proceeded to tell them the goldfish story and we all had a good laugh as we all lay on our backs and stared at the clouds flitting across the blue Sydney sky. We all laughed uproariously about the regurgitating goldfish, while their pooches bounded around us in great delight; then, with our stomachs full of hamburgers and fish and chips, it was time to do the wedding — they were so happy and it was 'just the sort of ceremony we wanted!' they said.

It was these couples who had their feet on the ground, and were appreciative that I was flexible in giving them the style of ceremony they had wanted. They sent a Christmas card every year after that until we moved away and lost touch.

* * *

Of all the guests, it was generally the Father of the Bride who was the alcoholic one, whether it was because they were so pleased to get the whining 'It's-all-about-me' daughter married off at last and she could become someone else's problem, or whether it was to make a statement about 'I'm the Father of the Bride' and that was a first class excuse to have a damned good drink, I could never quite work out but it was the FOB who breathed the most alcoholic fumes on The Big Day.

'P-P-P-Parker,' one poor stuttering FOB breathed down my neck, 'F-F-F-Frederick P-P-P-Parker; I'm the father of the b-b-b-bride.'

'Oh, well done!' I said smiling and turning to shake his hand, 'and you are Mrs Parker?' I asked the little whimsical figure dressed in pale lavender taffeta by his side.

'Yes, I'm Cynthia,' she smiled sweetly. 'So pleased to meet you. Shaz and Tim have told us so much about you.'

103

The Big Day

'Want to hear a g-g-g-good one?' asked Frederick Parker prodding me on the arm and leaning closer with a grin like a Cheshire cat.

'No dear,' interrupted Cynthia Parker. 'I shouldn't think Wendy would appreciate your kind of jokes dear,' she concluded.

'Love a good one,' I said trying to smooth things over. 'What is it?'

'Well,' started Frederick Parker, 'this f-f-f-family you see, are at the d-d-d-dinner table …'

'No Frederick, no! You are *not* to tell Wendy the dinner table one,' stammered Cynthia Parker.

'Well …' went on Frederick ignoring poor, frenzied, little Cynthia, 'if you don't like it you may leave, my d-d-d-dear …' With a horrified look, poor, sad-looking Cynthia in her little lavender number, slid off amongst the guests while Frederick Parker went on with his story and I became all ears. 'You s-s-s-see,' he said, leaning even closer, breathing alcoholic fumes into my face, 'this family were at the dinner table, and the son asks his father. "Dad, how many kinds of b-b-b-boobs are there?"

'The f-f-f-father sur-sur-surprised, looks up and answers: "Well s-s-s-son, there are three kinds of b-b-b-breasts. In her twenties a woman's b-b-b-breasts are like melons, round and f-f-f-firm. In her thirties and forties they're like p-p-p-pears — still nice but hanging a bit. After fifty — they're like onions."

'"Onions?" asked the b-b-b-boy.

'"Yes, one look at them and they make you c-c-c-cry."

'Well,' slurred Frederick Parker as he went on without stopping and starting to spit in my face, 'this made his wife and d-d-d-daughter very angry.'

'And then the d-d-d-daughter asked her mother: "Mother, how many w-w-w-willies are there?"

'The mother smiled and answered, "Well d-d-d-dear — a man goes through three phases as well. In his twenties. his w-w-w-willy is like an oak tree — f-f-f-firm and h-h-h-hard. In his thirties and forties it's a bit like a birch tree — f-f-f-flexible and reliable. And after his fifties, it goes like a C-C-C-Christmas tree."

"'A Christmas tree?' asked the d-d-d-daughter.

"'Yes,' said the mother, 'exactly like a C-C-C-Christmas tree — dead from the roots up and the b-b-b-balls are for decoration only!'"

With that Frederick Parker slapped me on the back and we both dissolved into peals of laughter, Frederick guffawing and spitting as he wiped his large red alcoholic face with his neatly ironed handkerchief.

'That's a good one,' I said when we had both calmed down a bit. 'I haven't heard that one before.'

'C-C-C-Cynthia hates it,' he went on. 'Says I'm like the C-C-C-Christmas tree after having a few drinks.' And with that final remark and again mopping his hot and sweaty forehead, Frederick Parker staggered away across the gardens to tell the same joke to the parents of the groom who stood staring at us poker-faced and who, I thought, definitely needed cheering up on such a happy occasion.

Chapter 6
Bloody Liars and Thieves

With the jokes came the whoppers — and whoppers don't always refer to breasts. Aussies call a lie a 'Porky Pie' but to be honest, nothing describes a 'whopper' better than the word 'lie', and lie many couples do. Before glassy-eyed couples walk into my office, naturally I aim to make a firm appointment. Surely that's not too hard to organise, as my doors are open from 9am-9pm, 7 days a week. At the eleventh hour as I sit watching the clock and waiting for the door buzzer to go, invariably the phone rings.

'Wendy, it's Kaz here; we had an appointment with you tonight at 6.30pm but my grandmother's just died, so we will have to reschedule.'

Hardly any emotion in Kaz's voice, and with the sound of much cheering and noise in the background I am picking that the local pub after work is better than organising the paperwork with the celebrant.

This is probably the most used lie I hear. 'Sorry,' says Maggie, 'but I forgot about the family Thursday night dinner; we'll have to reschedule.'

Maggie continues to point out that the family dinners have been a tradition for about ten years — yet she 'forgot' that Thursday nights are out? I know they were bloody liars because the majority always rang at the last minute which simply meant that something better than talking to the celebrant about the all-important ceremony had just cropped up. 'I've got to go to the hairdresser,' wailed one of them. 'It's Thursday night and I'll look a mess for my friend's engagement on Saturday if I don't get something done with it tonight.' From frock fittings, to dance lessons, from netball to taking the dog to the vet, I think I've had every appointment cancellation lie. 'I can't find my car keys,' bleated Bob, 'and I have to pick up the better half; we'll have to cancel out tonight.' Just another lie.

And then came, 'I've just broken the heel off my shoe, and anyway, I want to see the photographer as I'm spending thousands on him and I can't afford for him to make a mistake, can I?' 'The trains aren't running to Chatswood tonight,' complained one bride-to-be. Strange as I had only just stepped off the train myself and was racing back to my office to meet her.

* * *

Completing yet another pile of paperwork, I asked the obligatory question, 'Have you been married before?' to which the groom replied: 'No never, definitely not.' Well, that was good enough for me; after all, they signed a Declaration to say as much ... until the phone rang next day.

It was Lily, snivelling and sobbing into the phone. I could hardly understand what she was talking about.

'Wendy, it's Lily Chan here,' she sobbed. 'I can't believe it (sob) but Toby confessed (sob, sob) to me last night when we got home (sob, sniff) from your place (sniff, sniff) that he's been married before (sob, sob). What on earth do I do?'

'You'll have to get his divorce document from China and get it translated but you'll have to hurry; you've only got four weeks to get it.'

The divorce papers took six weeks to get to Sydney and another week to be translated, which meant calling all the pre-invited guests and delaying the wedding. Lily had seemed to take all this fairly well in her stride but was a mess by the time the wedding day arrived and Toby looked very sheepish throughout the entire ceremony, (as he should have).

And it wasn't until the vows were being repeated did the poor sobbing Lily finally and truly crack under the pressure.

'Toby,' she blurted out so loudly the whole of Chinatown could have heard, 'next time we get married, don't you *ever* do that to me again; don't you *ever* tell me you are *ever* divorced *ever* again!'

Next time? The horrified look of the guests' faces said it all.

* * *

There was often a next time but not necessarily to the same person unless of course they had previously divorced and then remarried but this didn't happen too often. Not too many Elizabeth Taylors thank goodness.

My most married groom admitted to five times and my most married bride was on to her fourth although I often suspect that many had missed out declaring a marriage or two, simply by the looks on their faces when I asked the all too awful question.

* * *

With the wind whistling around us and hair styles that just didn't exist in the biting cold air, the ceremony was, surprisingly under the ghastly conditions, going like clock-work. The divorced groom, proud to be standing next to his extremely beautiful and young new bride some 23 years younger, was a cradle snatcher by all accounts — but a proud one at that. Just as the bride and groom were exchanging their rings, a car screeched to a halt beside the park where we were standing under a massive fig tree, the car horn loudly honking to attract attention.

The guests and I all looked up to see what the commotion was all about, when suddenly from the rear door of the car, tumbled

The Big Day

three children under the age of about ten, yelling, 'Daddy, Daddy, we're here; we're coming.'

The three children, oblivious of the solemn marital occasion, threw themselves into the groom's arms much to the bewilderment and absolute horror of the beautiful, young and voluptuous bride. 'These are *yours*?' demanded the horrified, pale-faced bride, '*Yours*?' There was nothing the groom could say. The marriage plans had been leaked to the ex-wife from an inside source and with bitterness brimming from non-existent maintenance payments and determined to spoil her ex-husband's wedding day, she had decided this was one way she could finally pay him back and reap her own reward. It certainly had the desired effect.

* * *

Bigamy was the dreaded word! If discovered in a bigamous relationship, the responsible spouse would be landed with either a pretty hefty fine or a few weeks in Her Majesty's Motel. Alan was the confident self-assured groom and marrying Laura was to be the highlight of the year. With no expense spared, Laura and her mother had organised the perfect extravaganza wedding day, from the $9,000 photographer's package to the $1,400 three-tiered wedding cake. The white horses and carriage were a must and the white doves which were to fly off into the sunset as I declared Laura and Alan 'husband and wife' was all arranged with supposed, absolute precision. But was it Alan's conscience which got the better of him, or was this white meringue wedding just far too sickly sweet to stomach, on such a blistering hot Summer's day?

Just as Alan was to repeat his vows, he turned to me and said, 'Sorry Wendy, but I can't go through with it; I'm already married. Didn't tell you.' In all the years of being a celebrant, I have never seen such a horrified look on a bride's face. Her mouth opened and closed like a proverbial gold fish and not a sound did she utter.

'Come on guys,' he called to his groomsmen, who were all dressed up like penguins, 'let's get out of here — fast!' With that, the bride in all her pure white and glorious meringue let out a piercing scream, and hitching up her massive skirts and with her huge bosom heaving, raced after the groom across the lawn, smashing him over the head with her $600 bouquet. Flowers hung from the groom's head and shoulders as he tried to defend himself with as much dignity as he could allow but it was all too much.

The bride's mother also took flight and with her little jewel-covered shoulder bag she took aim at the groom who was by this time at the far end of the park. Those, who weren't stunned by the event, burst into laughter at such an amusing sight. The bride, returning to the crowd, was by this time, raging and fuming with anger.

'And you can all just fuck off,' she screamed at the guests before being led away by her distressed mother. 'Go on,' she continued, 'have your fucking laugh and then just fuck off.'

'I knew it wouldn't last,' I heard someone mutter. Strange how the 'Already Married' lie has such an effect.

* * *

Often I felt like a packhorse or mountain donkey carrying equipment across parks and gardens, over rocks and along soft sandy beaches, negotiating cliff paths and struggling through native bush. Eventually my trusted roadie, Philip, took on the job of driving and trudging, carrying and setting up, organising the bridal parties as they arrived and a million other roadie chores like getting the car topped up with petrol, checking tyres, making sure the amplifier batteries were charged and so on.

I even bought him a badge which said 'Celebrant's Assistant' so that guests would stop asking him whether he was related to

111

the bride or groom, because when they were true, feral families, you didn't want to be even, remotely or distantly related.

Scheduled for a wedding in the National Park, I asked the bride and groom at one of their appointments how far the ceremony area was from the car park.

'Not far,' lied the groom. 'Only a few metres.'

Good, nice and close I thought. It was hot and steamy, having rained the night before, as we set off through the bush following the yellow ribbons which had surprisingly, been very thoughtfully tied to trees so the guests and I didn't get lost. Strange how the few metres kept going on and on, through little puddles and pools from the previous rain, bushes scraping the sides of my pantihose and Philip trudging along in front carrying the amplifier, microphone, and briefcase while I carried the signing lectern. I swore I would kill anyone at this wedding who came up to me and said, 'What a wonderful job you've got; think I'll become a celebrant.' As we wended our way through the thick bush track, a long brown snake suddenly appeared from nowhere, but as quickly as it had come, it shot off back into the undergrowth. Thankfully it didn't display any venomous tactics. 'You didn't tell me we had to walk so far to get here,' I confronted the groom with as we arrived panting and staggering into the ceremony area, 'and we even saw a snake!'

'Well,' replied the groom, 'we thought you might not come if we actually told you how far it really was.'

After waiting nearly an hour for all the guests to finally find their way through the undergrowth, the ceremony got underway. Verses were read and prayers were said and Buddhist chanting created a truly magical moment.

Magical indeed for, just as it finished, the large brown snake appeared again, this time sitting up on his tail and spitting across at the guests who could do nothing but look on in sheer horror.

Never have I experienced such horror during a ceremony and the white ashen faces of the guests said it all.

Chapter 6 — *Bloody Liars and Thieves*

Again, for some unknown reason the snake turned as quickly as it had come and shot off back into the bush.

That was enough excitement for the day, and we literally ran back down the track to the car park and for good measure, even locked the car doors. I lost count of the number of times the couples lied to me over various things. On the way back to Sydney the clouds grew blacker and then it absolutely poured. 'Serves them right,' I thought. 'That'll teach you to lie, out in the bush with no cover, getting soaked to the skin. Serves you right!'

* * *

I always suggested to couples they invite their guests at least half an hour prior to the ceremony starting time, so that guests who had lost their way would actually arrive at the ceremony, had time to settle down, kiss and hug long lost or distant relatives, go to the loo, take the funny family flicks and tell me what a wonderful job I had. 'I think I'll become a celebrant, too,' they would say bright-eyed.

That extra half an hour was more often than not the most wonderful life saver and enabled me to schedule my day so much better.

But 'Madam It's-All-About-Me' did not arrive at the appointed time of 4 o'clock but rudely kept her guests, the photographer, the caterers and myself waiting for nearly an hour. I reminded the groom, 'I thought we'd arranged a 4 o'clock start?'

'No,' he replied with a supercilious Gen Y smirk, 'Cherie just wanted you to get here early; been to too many weddings where the celebrant doesn't rock up 'til late — it's really a 5 o'clock start.'

'I do have a schedule to keep — that's not really fair, is it?' I asked.

'Your problem,' retorted the groom as he turned his back on me and ambled off to speak with his guests. Couples thought they could book me for the whole day and that I had nothing

113

The Big Day

better to do than sit and wait for them. After all, it was *their* Big Day. Finally, with her haughty head held high and arriving with attitude plus, 'Madam It's-All-About-Me' made her appearance. But so much for the smirking groom who tells lies and 'Madam It's-All-About-Me,' for I heard on the grapevine the marriage lasted all of eleven months. The groom left her pregnant and with the mortgage which just happened to be in her name.

I was not surprised one little bit. As they say: what goes around comes around.

* * *

When I was first appointed I used to carry a signing table, two chairs, amplifier, microphone, briefcase and lectern. I often had to make two trips to the car and back to the ceremony area hauling equipment like Grace Bros Removalists.

One October afternoon as I was delivering the first load of equipment from my car across to the ceremony area, I heard the dreaded words, 'Think I'll become a celebrant.'

Looking up, I saw 'Madam' standing beside me decked out in her finest attire. 'Wonderful,' I replied, smiling. 'Let me show you what it's all about then — after the ceremony why not come and get some good old celebrant practice and help me carry all my equipment back to the car?'

I turned around but she had gone.

The stilettoed Madam had melted into the background as quickly as she had appeared at my side.

* * *

Before my trusted roadie's time, I recall asking a groomsman if he would mind helping carry the table back to the car. 'That'll be the day! Who do you think I am — a fucking furniture removalist?' was the reply.

Chapter 6 — *Bloody Liars and Thieves*

That was it. I learned never again to ask for help, ever again.

*　*　*

Many a time it was on the tip of my tongue to tell couples I wasn't a furniture removalist by trade but a marriage celebrant, yet I was often asked if I provided a CD player, amplifiers, red carpet, table, chairs, bridal arches, flowers and so on. I was quick to advise them to contact an Event Organiser. 'But we don't want to have to pay for all that sort of thing. Don't you provide all that?' would be the usual reply.

'I'm a marriage celebrant who is only really required to perform a legal role,' I'd tell them. 'We're not obliged to act as musicians or event hire people. We are only obliged to bring our own P.A. system. You must organise professionals to play music and event hire people to provide carpets and furniture if you want those extra services.

But I wish I could have said, 'I'm not a bloody furniture removalist, a musician or anything else you want me to be.'

You've got to pay for most things in life but if the wedding didn't teach them that then marriage certainly would: kids, the mortgage and all.

A groomsman once delighted in telling me of what he was going to say to the bride and groom in his speech.

'What's that?' I asked full of curiosity, waiting for the bride to arrive. 'Well, it goes like this,' he boasted. '"Daddy," asked the little boy of his father, "how much does it cost to get married?"

'"Dunno, son," replied the father, "but I guess I'm still paying for it — after all these years of being married to your mother."'

I couldn't imagine the guests laughing too long or too hard over that one. And then he came up with another: '"Is this true Dad? I heard in some parts of Africa a man doesn't know his wife until he marries her?"

'The father replied: "That happens in most countries, son."'

115

You never, ever really got to know your couples deep down and after all the ridiculous requests for carpets and so on, I'd think to myself of what they would be paying out for alcohol, food, music, photographer, dresses, suits, hair and makeup, cake, cars, flowers and of course the lavish honeymoon while the celebrant pocketed a minimal couple of hundred bucks compared to what they spent on other things. Olivia paid $1,200 just for her bouquet alone, $2,000 for her Jimmy Choo shoes and the cake was $1,900 but I don't think they ever remembered that they couldn't get married without a celebrant in the first place.

What it was to be just a commodity — or was I really only a suburban Post Office?

* * *

The liars never really ceased telling lies. After flouncing into my office flashing a brilliant sparkler, dragging her much younger trophy behind her, I asked the bride where the marriage was to be held.

'Oh, only about twenty minutes from the racecourse in Goulburn.'

Setting out with directions on the day, I discovered that twenty minutes should have been one hour and twenty minutes — minimum.

After reaching the small township of Taralga the map indicated a right turn.

Leaving the bitumen road way behind, I wended my way through native flora and fauna until I saw the yellow ribbon tied to a tree. I'd already travelled long past the 'only twenty minutes from Goulburn' instruction. We were by this time, as the crow flies, very much southwest of the Wombeyan Caves in the middle of nowhere. We continued on through virgin bush over tracks winding around dense scrub and fallen gum trees, which had never been sawn and cleared, but we still followed the yellow ribboned signs until a wisp of smoke on a distant hill indicated signs of life. As we neared the wedding site we caught the smell of cooking meat — never has lamb on the spit smelt so good!

I looked at my watch — two hours and ten minutes it had taken from the Southern Highlands, and I'm not a slow driver by a long shot.

'That's a fair way; a lot longer than twenty minutes from the race course,' I said to the groom as I got out of the car. 'So what do you think you're being paid for?' was his reply.

But the lack of courtesy and lies kept on coming, especially when it came to the paperwork. 'What town or city were you born in?' I asked the groom looking up from my paperwork.

'Calcutta,' he replied.

'But it says here in your passport you were born in 'The States'; have you got a birth certificate?'

'Yes, my grandmother has it in India,' was the reply. 'It's a mistake on the passport. I don't want your paperwork to say I was born in the States, I want it to say I was born in India.'

'Why?' I asked but I didn't get any response.

'Come on, where were you born? Your passport says the States and passport offices don't get this sort of thing wrong.'

'Well, I just don't want any of my paperwork to say I was born in the States; anyway, my mother will tell you I was born in India — and so will my grandmother,' was the answer.

'But I don't want to speak to your mother or your grandmother. I am asking you a plain question: where were you born?'

'I think I was born in India but my passport says the States.'

'You think? You remember being born?' I asked shooting him a look to wilt the freshest bouquet.

I gave up and told him he should stick to the truth and not try to get me to illegally change the paperwork, but to go and get married at Births, Deaths and Marriages instead, or come back when he could produce his birth certificate. I knew he would do neither and wiped my hands of yet another bloody liar.

* * *

The Big Day

'Crikey!' exploded one liar as I completed the Notice of Intended Marriage. 'You're asking if I've been married before!'

"Yes,' I replied, 'it's a question on the form which needs to be answered.'

The bride looked up from thumbing through my album of bridal photos.

'Well, go on Bud; answer Wendy; have you been married before?' demanded the bride-to-be.

'Well …' stuttered the groom.

'So you *have*,' shrieked the bride catching the faltering groom. 'I knew it, I just knew it; well you can bloody get lost!'

And grabbing her handbag off my office desk, she made for the door, slamming it firmly shut behind her. Yes, they even lied to each other.

* * *

Offering to perform the ceremony in my apartment often relieved the couples of having to find a venue for the wedding and provided a roof — in case of intense heat or pouring rain — but I always stressed a maximum of ten people.

Even *that* was too many in my apartment but I figured out ten although cramped, was a reasonable number. The buzzer went from downstairs. Janine and Rob had arrived, so I pressed the intercom to let them in. Imagine my horror as I opened my apartment door which led into the corridor, to be confronted by no less than 50 guests.

'How are you all going to fit in here?' I asked Janine as she swept past me, in her champagne meringue, veil and all.

'Easy,' replied Janine. 'I knew if I told you there would be more than ten guests you wouldn't let us get married here, so I lied — simple as that. We'll fit. Don't worry. Come on guys, come in; Wendy won't mind.'

Chapter 6 — *Bloody Liars and Thieves*

Talk about packing them in like sardines; they even stood in the kitchen peering over the buffet and outside on the balcony looking in through the glass doors.

*　*　*

They even lied about their names until I checked birth certificates; in fact some were so dumb they didn't even know their parents' correct names and would lie as I completed the paperwork.

'It says here on your Birth Certificate that your mother's first name is Pamela; you told me it was Frances,' I stated looking across at the bride.

'Did I?' responded the bride nonchalantly, thumbing through a bridal magazine on my desk. 'We all lie about Mum's name even though she hasn't changed it legally. No one ever doubts us; just put Frances on the form, Wendy,' she instructed. 'Well she hates the name Pamela … does it matter?'

Another 'porky pie' — and I didn't do as she asked. Her legal name was Pamela and that was that.

*　*　*

A lovely couple came not long afterwards and as I completed the paperwork, I asked, 'Are any of your parents deceased?'

'Yes, mine are,' replied the groom. 'Long since gone, thank God.'

So it was a huge surprise to be confronted by Joe and Tina Papadopoulos alive and kicking, on the day of the wedding. Certainly not deceased.

'Why did you tell me your parents were deceased?' I asked the groom quietly drawing him aside.

'Because I can't stand either of them and that's where they should be — dead and bloody buried, under the bloody lilies,' he

119

snarled. Another lie. So when I got back to my office, for obvious reasons, I altered the paperwork.

*　*　*

In all my years as a celebrant, I have never been late for a wedding. Having taught Time Management, I always lived by the adage of 'practise what you preach'. A professional celebrant knows the importance of punctuality and is never, ever late. Ever.

One cold Autumn afternoon, we turned up to a wedding at Richmond, arriving at the house with plenty of time to spare but the usual line-up of cars was not parked out on the road nor was there any answer from my knock on the front door.

Going around to the back of the house, I discovered everything laid out for a wedding reception but still no sign of life except for two big dogs, who wagged their tails in delight as I gave each a pat. I tried calling mobiles but as per usual they were turned off, so I scrambled through the hedge and went and knocked next door.

Taking some time to appear, an almost naked man with a blue towel wrapped around his middle answered the door.

'Just wondered whether you knew where everyone next door's gone for the wedding,' I asked.

'No idea — not invited,' he responded. 'Heard all their cars take off about half an hour ago.' I had no alternative but to sit in the car outside the front of the house and wait until someone came looking for me which happened about half an hour later. 'We wondered where you were,' said the groom leaning out the car window. 'Get lost?'

'No, been here an hour,' I answered. 'You told me the wedding was to be at the house at 10am.'

'Oh no, we were never going to do that; it's down by the river. Knew you probably wouldn't do it down there — bit of a hike through the bush with all your equipment and stuff,' continued the groom.

'Tried to call your mobile but it's switched off,' I said. 'You should have been honest with me.'

'Can't tell you everything,' was the reply. 'Should've worked it out for yourself.' And yet another lie, for I had been distinctly told it was to be at the house and to be there at 10am for a 10.30am start.

* * *

After a couple flew from Egypt to marry in Sydney, I mailed them photos but they were returned from both addresses I had been given, marked as 'Not Known at This Address'.

And why could I only ever contact them through a friend's email address? They didn't even have their own Hotmail address and being professional people … made me wonder. Another lie about where they lived or who they were perhaps, but their paperwork checked out and they were married 'all above board'. Oh well, c'est la vie.

* * *

And so it went on year after year.

'And your date of birth?' I asked the elderly, well-groomed lady seated at my desk.

'8th January, 1936,' she replied, 'yes, 1936.'

She seemed to be reassuring herself.

'I will of course, need to see your birth certificate before you get married,' I told her.

'But I can't possibly show you that,' she replied looking worried. 'It's lost, years ago; got lost when we moved house.'

The Big Day

'Well, I'm afraid, Betty, you're going to have to get a copy. As you were born here in Sydney, here's a form — they're easy enough to get. Just take some ID as it explains on the back cover.'

Betty and Tom left my office armed with the appropriate form, Betty returning on her own, just prior to the wedding with a copy of her birth certificate.

'It says here, Betty, you were born in 1926,' I quizzed.

'Oh Wendy, please don't put 1926 on the paperwork. I told Tom I am only 70. If I tell him I'm 80 he probably won't marry me. Anyway, it says I was born in 1936 on my driver's licence; won't that do?'

'Afraid not Betty,' I sympathised. 'Now come on. You don't want to spend a week in Her Majesty's Motel, do you?'

I tried to make light of the matter to ease the tension I could see cross over Betty's face.

'No,' sighed Betty, 'and I probably wouldn't get my driver's licence as easily if I told them my real age.'

'Didn't they ask to see your birth certificate when you got your licence?' I asked.

'Oh no, not in those days; they just trusted us to tell the truth.' I wonder to this day, how many over 80-year-old grey nomad grannies are driving around Australia, living the delicious lie.

* * *

But not only did they lie, they stole. Just about to disconnect the microphone from my amplifier, I looked up to see the Mother of the Bride stuff my beautiful silver antique ring dish into her handbag.

'Excuse me,' I smiled, 'but that belongs to me.'

'Oh … I thought that was included in the fee,' she lied, putting it back on the table with a loud thump and walking away. Another time, I turned to take the tablecloth and candlesticks off a little table that I had provided for the ceremony, but my rather expensive white linen cloth and the candle sticks had already been whisked from the table, and were both long since gone. That was the last time I ever took anything like that to a wedding ceremony. I now just take my lectern and P.A. system and hope that they don't walk.

I lost verse books and CDs to couples who swore they'd never borrowed them until I asked them to sign for them but eventually it was only my word against theirs that they had returned them, so I gave up lending.

Silver signing pens also walked, as did the verse books. I recall that once, soon after repairing my lipstick, I turned around to see a young girl snatch it back out of my briefcase and stuff it down her bra. A musician I hadn't met before pretended he thought my amplifier was his, as he hurriedly walked away from the ceremony area. Thankfully, I inherited a very loud voice from my school teacher mother, so I got it back but just in time as he tried to duck behind a large Moreton Bay fig tree at Rushcutters Bay Park.

* * *

They lied and they stole, and worse, brimmed to the hilt with attitude, they thought I was stupid enough to believe them and that I wouldn't miss anything which disappeared or believe their lies as they looked you straight in the eye and spoke with total conviction.

I always kept a very close eye on my briefcase, luckily that stayed and never vanished but I guess there's always a first time. A huge pre-requisite of being a marriage celebrant is not only do you need two pairs of eyes in the back of your head at all times otherwise what *should* be under your nose won't be there next time you turn around but you also need to let the lies go in one ear and out the other unless they are to do with legalities. A bit like the clown at the circus who constantly turns from side to side, with ping pong balls being stuffed down its throat, continually watching but mostly gagged. Or like the three wise monkeys — see no evil, speak no evil, hear no evil.

Chapter 7
Location, Location, Location

'Feral Farm' was exactly that. Feral. The name was painted on the front fence of the small property and the house lived up to its name. I couldn't help but smile at their honesty. Two rust buckets sat side by side on the front lawn with grass growing up around their sides and a strange collection of yapping dogs raced around in the excitement. 'And who are youse?' asked a large tattooed man in his early twenties leaning against the front door, looking us up and down.

'The marriage celebrant,' I replied offering to shake his hand, but the feral one wasn't in the mood. We were in sharp contrast to him and he didn't like it.

'Probably the cops,' he said distrustfully looking around, 'anyway youse are early,' he said ignoring my hand, 'may as well come in — if you can.' 'If you can' meant walking sideways up the front passage, squeezing in between boxes of junk stacked against its side walls and stepping over the unemptied cat litter trays near the kitchen.

'Tracey's in the bedroom getting done over,' offered the tattooed one as we edged our way through the junk, 'and Chaz is still under the shower.'

I translated 'done over' as having her makeup and hair done so I just called out to Tracey through the closed bedroom door and told her I'd wait out the back yard until they were ready to come out for the ceremony.

So along with a dozen or so other hooded ferals dressed to kill in ripped jeans, covered in tats and adorned with earrings, we all waited with as much patience as we could possibly muster until Tracey and Chaz made their entrance out to the Hills Hoist, an hour later. I performed many a ceremony under the old rusty Aussie Hills Hoist, generally beside a barbecue, for some reason they always seemed to sit side by side.

The Hills Hoist wouldn't have all been such a bad backdrop, I thought, provided the month old washing hanging limply around its sides had been taken in.

'Feral Farm' didn't disappoint. Chaz's old stained daks hung limply next to a couple of old checked shirts which wasn't the best sight on a hot Saturday afternoon, especially when you're surrounded by a dozen hooded ferals and their mates.

But like names were the locations — they were many and varied, and with real estate it's all about 'location, location' and with weddings, many times it is wisely chosen however, many times it was not. Of course it's the lies that seeped through the big vision but dream on beautiful bride about having your wedding on a beautiful beach except in reality, coping with kids and dogs, topless bathers, a rogue Spring tide, barbecues, intense heat with the sides of your feet burning around the edge of your strappy shoes and your floaty white dress with its soggy wet train. 'Is the wedding to be on the grass verge?' I'd ask them.

'Yes, on the grass,' they'd lie. 'Oh good, because it's very hard for guests, especially grandmas to walk on the sand in their pantihose and heels,' I'd say offering the hugest hint. On The Big Day you'd usually find the wedding was set up down on the beach anyway, without any apologies to anyone. The more mature guests would be standing up on the grass verge with looks of horror on their faces, firmly refusing to budge. I mean, who in their right mind expects their guests to trudge down onto the sand getting it in their shoes, socks and pantihose? And sand between the feet and strappy shoes — agony!

Chapter 7 — *Location, Location, Location*

Oh worse — burnt soles when it's 38 degrees in the shade.

Whoops, I nearly forgot the bride's cliché, 'It's all about *me*.' It usually took an enormous amount of coaxing to get guests to walk down to the sea shore but eventually they would struggle down onto the sand in their smart wedding numbers with shoes in hand, so the ceremony could commence. How I hate beach weddings.

At Freshwater Beach one Spring tide morning, the usual lie prevailed.

'Yes, we're having it up on the grassy area,' I'd been told, 'just near the restaurant.'

Wrong again, I should have known better than to believe them.

Another lie. It's a fairly steep sort of track that leads down to the beach from the south end of Freshwater, so down we struggled with the obligatory lectern, briefcase, amplifier and microphone.

'I thought you said the ceremony was to be up on the grass?' I enquired.

Now I wonder why I honestly thought I'd get a truthful answer to that one. Finally but finally, the guests struggled down the path and across the sand and we were able to begin the ceremony.

Suddenly a voice, 'Hey!' and looking up, saw someone in a wheelchair at the top on the grassy cliff waving frantically.

'You'd better go up and help him down,' I volunteered. 'Oh, he'll be right,' replied the ignorant groom looking up at the poor guest, 'he can wheel himself down all right.'

'But that path is so steep, he can't possibly wheel himself down there, let alone across soft sand,' I told him.

'Course he can, let him find his own way,' snorted the groom. A couple of well-meaning guests went up and helped the wheelie bloke down to the sandy beach but to this day I have never seen even the most clever of wheelies, able to negotiate their

127

wheelchair down a steep track and then through soft sand on a beach.

Talk about ignorance and an insult to the disabled guest.

It wasn't just wheelchairs in sand that became problems it was the grandmas' and grandpas' twisted ankles which became the great threat and I twice called an ambulance because of the inconsideration shown to the elderly. One guest who'd travelled all the way from Germany fell and broke his leg when he was negotiating the top of a slimy rock surface which we all had to clamber over to get to the 'wedding area' which was inside a sandy cave. But no-one thought about checking the incoming tide and we all just made it out before being washed out to sea. Great location, that one. Thank heavens for mobile phones. Three trusty ambulance officers came quickly and did a remarkable job wading through the rising tide soaked to their knees, their feet sinking in the soft tidal sand at every step while the poor German moaned and wailed, leg in a splint and him being tied securely to the stretcher. Never thought I'd see a German cry at a wedding, but they do, especially when they've just broken a leg attending a wedding and being so far away from home with no travel insurance.

Trains and dresses also became saturated in the rising tides, and sand in your eyes is nothing but excruciating. Not to mention my amplifier and the lectern which wouldn't sit well on the sand, and when I had musicians turn up with their instruments — well, that's when the music really started as many refused to go onto a beach and expose their expensive instruments to the forces of Mother Nature of which I didn't blame them one little bit. At Whale Beach instead of the grassy area as planned, another ceremony was destined for the extreme northern end of the beach. Talk about yet another lie and a trudge with all the equipment. Never again — and I threatened every future bride and groom that if they changed their plans and wanted to get married on the sand, I would not budge from the grass verge, no matter how much they bribed me.

Chapter 7 — *Location, Location, Location*

Many times over the years, I was asked, 'where's the most unusual place you've ever done a wedding?' The 'location' question always reared its ugly head.

It was indeed unusual to find 40-odd guests, and me, standing on a wharf up at Pittwater while the couple bobbed up and down in their wetsuits beside us to say their vows but insisted on exchanging rings underneath the water which thankfully went without a hitch. Neither ring landed on the ocean floor, which was a great relief.

Years ago, I earned my private pilot's licence, learning on a little Piper Cherokee and on a gem of a Tiger Moth and to this day, nothing excites me more or makes the adrenalin flow, than being up above the clouds in almost anything that has wings.

My 'most unusual' but absolute favourite is always in a sleek Lear Jet skimming over the Sydney skyline. Of course the celebrant sits on a comfy padded seat at the very rear which is actually the toilet when the need arises. But it's always such a thrill to see the bride walk up an actual aisle in a plane. Helicopters are also a great passion, with brilliant visibility despite the noise but never did I tempt the skydiving or harbour bridge walk weddings which came my way.

I was asked once to marry a couple underneath the Harbour Bridge — in a wetsuit, of course. My roadie answered the phone and spoke on my behalf. No, his wife didn't perform weddings at the bottom of Sydney Harbour.

Sorry about that. Of course, I couldn't refuse to go up in a dear old DC3 from Camden Airport which sucked in pollen as we flew over the Southern Highlands right in the middle of the April winds. I wasn't the only one to exit the plane sneezing and with eyes watering.

But driving halfway back to Sydney, my breathing suddenly just got too difficult and my swollen eyes started to close.

'This is no good,' I thought, so I diverted into the Royal North Shore Hospital on my way back up the Highway to Chatswood.

129

By this time I was nearly passing out and my throat was swollen and all nasal passages totally blocked. Rushing into Emergency and pointing to my throat and blotchy skin, they swung me straight onto a bed and in went the drips and drugs, and under the oxygen mask I went. The Royal North Shore Emergency saw me for a second time not long afterwards when I decided to eat shellfish which I reacted badly to. Off we raced up the Pacific Highway at 4am on a Sunday morning and again back onto the bed with drips, tubes and a mask. By 7am I was feeling a lot better and breathing was easier but they insisted I stay in for a minimum of five hours but I had a wedding to perform at 11am at Balmoral Beach (on the grass!) and I needed time to go home, shower, wash my hair, change and travel and in all the years of being a celebrant, nothing was ever going to stop me performing a ceremony I'd booked nor was I ever going to be a 'late' celebrant. The hospital doctor argued my point, so finally I discharged myself and we raced home to get ready. High on hospital medication and feeling decidedly spaced out and light-headed, I got to Balmoral in the nick of time but kept turning the pages over wrongly and missed getting the bride to say her vows.

After trying to focus on a body full of hospital drugs and struggling through the legal parts for the second time to make sure they were definitely legally married and with the paperwork signed, my roadie drove me home and I spent the next 24 hours flat on my back, trying to regain some sort of normality in my life.

Talk about 'Location, location' and 'What ze French want, then ze French 'ave'. A gorgeous couple turned up to do the paperwork, declaring, 'Ve are from France and ve vant to get married under ze vashing line; I zink you call it ze Aussie Hills Hoist.'

And so, the adorable couple repeated their vows — in yet in another overgrown backyard — at their rented house in Randwick, to the tune of their small, white, yapping dog and under the Hills Hoist Aussie icon.

Chapter 7 — *Location, Location, Location*

Good on ze French!

The Shakespeare Room in the Sydney Library is a great little venue for those of the learned variety, as is the Art Gallery Foyer but the Museum of Sydney leaves me a bit mortified. Performing a ceremony between a Tyrannosaurus Rex and a rigid, stuffed tiger who met his untimely death in the depths of Africa after which he met up with a taxidermist, doesn't do anything to add to a romantic marriage ceremony.

Of course Sydney Harbour is a very special place with its brilliant views but not so nice on a windy day, when you're in a tiny little yacht with the boom swinging around above your head. One clunk or 'boom' and you're 'man overboard' so I learned to sit low and stay low, while the bride floated around above me in her billowing number yelling her vows above the screeching wind, ducking and diving under the boom, as she did.

Stupid place for the nuptials, hardly the most romantic venue when you come to think of it and the romance of the day soon flies out the porthole when the paperwork lands down on the harbour floor.

* * *

Siobhan was from Ireland and had flown all the way to Sydney, and then travelled on down to the Southern Highlands to marry in the beautiful grounds of Peppers Resort.

But it gets cold down there in late July and the icy winds sweep down from the Snowy Mountains, across the Tablelands and over the Southern Highlands in all their fury. Each year a few days of snow follow the icy winds and hit Bowral and the surrounding townships, laying its beautiful white carpet across the countryside. But not so beautiful on the day Siobhan was to marry. It was icy cold and the wind cut through you like a sharp, cold knife. I rugged up in my thick Winter coat over layers of underwear and a thick Winter suit and headed off for the resort.

131

The Big Day

By the time I got there it had started to sleet and I ran for the open log fire in the Great Hall.

All the guests were hunched over it in the bitter cold shivering like crazy trying to keep warm, so I went upstairs to the bridal suite to see the bride.

'It's just started to snow,' I told her, 'Siobhan have you a wrap for your shoulders? It's freezing downstairs.'

'Oh, I'll be fine,' replied Siobhan in her Irish sing-song voice, 'I'm used to all this sort of weather. But downstairs? No, we're definitely having the ceremony outside in the garden,' she concluded.

'But I can't even see where the garden begins and ends,' I told her, 'it's snowing.' There was no trying to change Siobhan's mind about having the ceremony beside the huge fireplace in the Great Hall. Siobhan insisted we all go out into the sleet and snow with the icy winds screaming around our poor frozen bodies. Snow doesn't discriminate but leaves a smooth white blanket across every path and garden in its wake, so it was no use even trying to determine where the paths and gardens started and finished. Eventually Siobhan arrived slipping and sliding down what she could just make out to be the path, as she approached, shivering like I have never seen a bride shiver, in her strapless shantung silk gown and with goose bumps as big as anthills on her arms, chest and back.

And because there's no telling where the wedding lawn actually was, we all ended up standing in the middle of a soggy snowy garden bed doing the ceremony.

Glad I'd remembered my gumboots in the boot of the car — you don't live in the Highlands without owning a trusty pair of these. But a celebrant soon learns that what a bride sets her heart on is what she wants and gets on her wedding day, and of course they seldom allow for a change of plans; as usual, the bride thinks she knows best. I called Siobhan a few days later as they were honeymooning in Sydney.

Chapter 7 — *Location, Location, Location*

I had promised I'd deliver her registered marriage certificate to their hotel. But Siobhan was too ill to come to the phone. For the past three days she had taken to her bed and not moved an inch, and according to Patrick, the doctor had refused to allow her to fly home to Ireland as she was so ill with pneumonia.

Location was of paramount importance to most couples, especially the reception venue.

* * *

Late one February afternoon, a very lengthy ceremony had meant that almost 200 guests had stood in the hot sun for two hours before they staggered back to their cars to journey across the city, from the ceremony area in the Royal Botanic Gardens to the function venue in Leichhardt.

The venue had been chosen because of its excellent reputation and fine food, plenty of guest parking and one which could seat their 200 guests with ease. But imagine the horror when the 200 guests arrived at the wedding reception to discover the doors locked. This was one wedding reception that definitely wasn't going to go ahead.

I heard later that someone in the office had written the wrong date in the bookings book — it had been written in by mistake for the following week.

All this resulted in one furious and thirsty lot of guests and one newly married couple who are still in the throes of a court case with the function centre.

They told me they had no alternative but to go down to the local RSL club who sympathetically agreed to get the chef to deep fry up a few hundred spring rolls and dim sums from the freezer while the guests ordered house reds and jugs of beer at the bar. Thank goodness celebrants can't take the rap for these venue errors, except couples do have the habit of changing their ceremony times and dates without telling you until the

133

The Big Day

night before when you ring them to confirm the plans for their wedding next day.

Celebrants are also meant to be mind readers and clairvoyants, all rolled into one.

Perhaps the Pink Fairy with her crystal ball could have helped out on some of these occasions.

Having just parked my car, down in a car park in Macquarie Street I was crossing the road over to the Rose Gardens, when my mobile went.

'Wendy, it's Shane,' said the groom, 'we've had a real bugger of a morning; the cars never turned up.'

'Where are you coming from?' I asked.

'Campbelltown,' he replied, 'but it gets worse.'

'What do you mean it gets worse?' I asked.

'Well, when the cars we booked and paid for never turned up, I called another car company who sent over two old convertibles. Well, the problem is they both ran out of petrol on the M5 so we are here now on the side of the road waiting for the NRMA to come and fill us up.' Looking at my watch I saw that the wedding was scheduled to begin in half an hour and I could see guests already arriving.

'You'll never make it on time, Shane,' I said, 'how long will the NRMA take to come?'

'Dunno,' replied Shane, 'there's five of us guys and we're all cooking in these stupid bloody suits.'

'Well, there's nothing anyone can do then,' I said reassuringly, 'just get here as soon as you can.' After waiting for one hour with 80 bored and very hot guests in the Rose Gardens, I called Shane again.

'What's happening Shane?' I asked, 'where are you?'

'Well, the NRMA came but now we're lost because these car guys have never driven into the city before, we're down some tunnel somewhere, I think near Moore Park.'

'Stay on the phone Shane,' I told him, 'and I'll talk you through it.'

Chapter 7 — *Location, Location, Location*

So with Shane saying, 'I can see a signpost that says William Street exit' and me saying, 'turn left, turn right' they eventually got to St Mary's Cathedral.

'Find Macquarie Street,' I called, 'you'll see a statue of Prince Edward on the corner.'

But the driver missed the turning into Macquarie Street and headed down towards David Jones in Elizabeth Street and getting caught up in the right hand lane, was forced to go all the way down to the bottom of Market Street to Darling Harbour. Julie was livid. It was a scorcher — 37 degrees in the shade and she and the girls had sat in their bridal car for nearly two and a half hours before the groomsmen eventually turned up at the Palace Gates.

The generally placid-natured Shane, who had tried his utmost not only to keep calm but had pulled out all stoppers with the NRMA and drivers of the old convertibles, told the driver in no uncertain terms, 'Fuck off mate! I never want to set eyes on youse again and,' he advised, 'get yourself a fucking Sydney road map or GPS because you couldn't fight your fucking way out of a fucking paper bag if you fucking tried.' Dream on beautiful bride; unfortunately lots can go wrong on The Big Day. Even the best laid plans of mice and men …

So off I went to another lovely little wedding with only the two witnesses which was to be held at their home overlooking the beach. The bride greeted me at the door dressed in a patterned orange dress; she looked lovely — a nice little casual number. The lounge room was divided in half; both the lounge room and the bedroom shared the same view for it was just the one room. It was then I noticed the bedspread was exactly the same material as the bride's dress, so after the ceremony I asked the bride to sit on the end of the bed while I took their photo for my album. The photo looked brilliant and takes pride in my album of pics.

Nothing like making the most of a few extra metres of fabric from Spotlight.

The Big Day

Early in my celebrant's career I arrived at a charming little house in Glebe, the couple's two large dogs wagging their tails furiously seemed happy to greet me. 'They're our babies,' the groom explained, 'mind if we have them with us during the ceremony?'

So we all sat down, the witnesses at the kitchen table, the bride and groom and their two huge dogs on the sofa while I was relegated to the rocking chair. It was the only time I performed a ceremony while rocking gently to the boredom of saying the Monitum and then hear the couple say their vows.

Amazing where one can perform a ceremony, even on the edge of a picnic rug. Well, almost. Upon arriving at Little Manly Park, I saw a middle-aged couple enjoying a picnic right where the couple had booked for their ceremony.

I politely explained to them that a couple had booked this area for their wedding, I had an authorisation form and asked if they would please mind moving somewhere else.

'Oh no luv,' said the woman haughtily. 'We're not movin', are we luv?' she addressed her husband.

'No luv, we're from Yorkshire and the views is what we want 'ere, i'n't it luv?'

'Oh aye luv, and we're not movin' — this is free public speece and we're here and we're not movin' are we luv?'

'Sorry,' I said, 'I am able to call the ranger to verify the wedding is due if you won't move.'

The couple completely ignored my statement and went on tucking into their little pork pies.

'Ok' I said lightly with a slight wry smile on my face, 'you stay and have your picnic and we'll have the wedding on the edge of your picnic rug.' Just about to call the ranger, I saw the groom and his groomsmen sauntering across the grass towards us. Never have I been more thankful to welcome five hugely tattoo-covered, unshaven blokes with earrings glittering from their noses and ears in the sunlight, hiding their alcoholic remorse behind dark sunnies.

Chapter 7 — *Location, Location, Location*

The sight was never truly more welcome, and the couple from Yorkshire who had refused my request to leave, couldn't pack up their picnic basket quickly enough and make a hasty retreat across the park.

And so from picnics to pot. Arriving at a large and popular beach side hotel to the obvious odour of pot, which hung around like the proverbial bad smell, didn't seem like too good a start.

Three hundred guests from right around Australia and a large Kiwi contingent milled around in the foyer, spilling out onto the street. The groom had tried to round them all up before I had arrived and the poor bride was beside herself waiting in the change room but the guests all refused to budge.

Eventually after about half an hour after the agreed starting time and with the help of my roadie we got underway and eventually, the paperwork was signed. At last they were legally married.

The Best Man certainly didn't turn out to be the best man on this occasion and ended up totally paralytic back out on the street front, so the groom asked if I could take over and be their MC for the night, which I said I'd do, just to help things run more smoothly than they otherwise would have gone.

I have never seen so much food piled high on buffet platters — prawns, oysters, lobster and so on and 300 people determined to have their fill.

Food and people were everywhere, at their tables, on the floor, in the foyer and some even eating out on the street and enjoying a drag in between each mouthful. About to commence the evening's speeches, I decided to round up the bridal party and guests and somehow try and get them back into the function room.

Whilst I attacked the foyer and street front, my roadie made for the men's toilets only to be confronted with ladies underwear and shoes showing out from under each toilet door. A good time was certainly being had by all.

The Big Day

It is not just the Kiwis but also the Irish who know how to party, and party they did, especially in Berrima at a wedding I was booked in for at 4pm on a lovely Spring Saturday afternoon. Arriving at the Inn at 3.30pm, the manager told me that the bride, groom and guests had all been over at the local pub since opening time in the morning and, 'if you can get them back for the wedding you're a better person than I am,' he told me. Apparently the manager had been over to the pub to try and round them up about half an hour before I had arrived but they were there to stay, or so they thought.

The groom, with his shirt hanging out and looking extremely dishevelled, had had a few drinks and the bride fell around in all her bridal glory, her breasts fighting to stay inside her dress, but between the guests and me, we managed to haul everyone back across the road and into the ceremony area.

I delayed the ceremony for nearly an hour and a half while the manager and I forced copious cups of coffee into the very happy bride, groom and their guests — and eventually, under a flowery bridal arch, I solemnised the marriage. While the photographer took the couple around the gardens for the all-important bridal pics after the ceremony the guests went back across the road for another pint, as the sun set in the west across Joadja way, out the back of the Old Hume Highway.

Of course the Southern Highlands is simply a magical place and there are so many beautiful locations to get married in, especially at Tulip Time in Bowral. Not that the Tulip Time Committee or Council rangers ever knew I performed ceremonies there when the tulips were in full bloom, so we'd plan the ceremony at sun-rise or sun-set before the people on the gates and busloads of tourists arrived or disappeared, and we'd all stand amongst the tulips listening appropriately to Tiny Tim's, 'Tip Toe Through the Tulips' as the bride made her entrance. Some requested 'Tulips from Amsterdam' but a Dutch friend, assured me there were no tulips in Amsterdam itself, but despite this we always enjoyed listening to it because somehow it seemed appropriate and suited the occasion. Many a time we had to clamber over the little picket fence because the gates were locked.

And I'm glad that no-one thought to take a pic to capture the ungainly moment of the Celebrant climbing over the picket fence in her long black skirt.

I often felt though, I should have donned my bright yellow Dutch clogs for the occasion.

And I also thought it appropriate never to ask the bride where her bouquet of tulips came from either; I just used to let that one slide.

Another beautiful wedding and another perfect moment as a couple became husband and wife. I shall always love my Tulip Time weddings.

* * *

As the sun set, so did the candles flicker in Newtown. A whole house full of beautiful flickering candles, on the mantelpiece, on the bookcases, on the edge of the stairs, in fact anywhere there was room to put one.

I asked the bride how many candles she'd lit — 493, the number of days they had known each other. What a glorious sight and such a beautiful ambience it gave, but I dreaded to think how much wax would need to be scraped up of the polished floorboards the following day, as they melted their hearts out in the Sydney Summer heat.

From pub beer gardens to back yards with the old Hills Hoist adorned with the likes of Chaz's daks, I performed the ceremony of marriage. Whilst we were living down near Robertson in the Southern Highlands, our local Country Show was always held each year in March, but at that time, the fog's generally as thick as Grandma's pea soup. 'Wanna get married on the back of me ute,' Baz informed me, 'just before the Demolition Derby; me and Bea think that'd be great.'

'Yes,' continued Bea looking all excited, 'and that way we don't have to have a proper wedding reception 'cos all our friends'll be at the show anyway.'

'They can all get pissed at the bar on our behalf and at their expense,' grinned Baz.

The weather kept its promise, for on Baz and Bea's Big Day, visibility was about three metres and even the Demolition Derby had to be cancelled because no-one could see what was going on, even worse for the drivers who drove backwards through the whole race until their vehicle was a total smashed up wreck and refused to go.

'So what's Plan B,' I asked, 'if the fog's low?'

'We'll just do it in the shed,' Baz said.

So the nuptials were performed in between the preserved jams and prize pumpkins, while in the kitchen, the ladies from the CWA polished off the last of the day's home-baked scones.

Hyde Park produced a real attraction. I warned the couple that 5 o'clock may not be an appropriate time for their ceremony as Saturday Mass at St Mary's Cathedral was always at 5pm but the bride explained that it didn't matter, they'd take full advantage of the free bells which tolled to announce both the Mass and also their own ceremony.

About a minute to 5 o'clock, as the bells started to toll, three large tourist buses pulled up near the church steps, their doors expelling a mass of Asian tourists who raced up the stairs to attend Mass. Incredibly though, one tourist had turned around and in the distance, had spotted our wedding grouped together and I could hardly believe what happened next.

The whole three bus-loads of tourists stopped dead in their tracks at the top of steps and following the lead of the tourist who had seen us, they all raced back down, ducking and diving through the traffic as they crossed College Street and across into

Chapter 7 — *Location, Location, Location*

Hyde Park to the Sandringham Gardens and to our wedding. And there, with an extra hundred or so uninvited guests watching, I performed the ceremony much to the cheering and delight of them all. Cameras clicked as they posed unashamedly alongside the bride and groom and as the ceremony concluded they all raced back across College Street to board their buses. So much for attending the sanctity of Mass.

Mrs Macquaries Chair was also a favourite for tourists to enjoy a wedding but eventually I warned couples of the tourist invasion which was likely to occur.

It was almost impossible at times to ask tourists to move back away from the ceremony as they seemed to want to touch the brides dress and veil and be in every possible photo.

I have even had tourists stroking my blonde hair at the back, while I've been performing a ceremony because blonde hair is such a novelty in the country from which they're from.

One Saturday I arrived an hour early for a wedding at Mrs Macquaries Chair so I could get a car park close to the point and counted 35 buses pulling up, exhuming its inhabitants who raced out to the little lookout point, taking photos of the Harbour Bridge and Opera House, then with a quick uninvited pose with myself, the bride and groom, they clambered back on board only to be whisked off to their next destination to hold a koala or buy another tacky souvenir which was probably made in China anyway.

But they'd been to an Aussie wedding and to prove it they had their pics.

'We're getting married at the SCG,' announced one bride happily, 'we've got a private box for the night, the Swans are playing, and we're all mad Swans' fans.'

What a great way to get married, I thought, all wearing red and with a fun legal ceremony at half-time, and enjoying every last drop of the red. So with 40,000 odd guests this ranked as my second largest wedding.

The 'largest' wedding was on a New Year's Eve and was an absolute delight — a wedding at five minutes to midnight and as I declared them husband and wife on the stroke of twelve, the champagne flowed and fireworks exploded from the Harbour Bridge.

'Where are you getting married?' I had asked the couple. 'In the upper forecourt at the Opera House, we'll get you a Security Pass — meet us outside Door Number Five as we're going to the concert first, then we'll go straight outside onto the forecourt and you can do the ceremony just before the fireworks go off!' So with just under a million 'guests' and with only their two witnesses, their little ceremony at the Opera House forecourt went like clockwork and at two minutes to midnight, and us with our glasses of champagne and with the fireworks exhibiting their amazing display as the New Year rolled in, I declared them 'husband and wife'.

It took us nearly three hours to get back to Chatswood in the early hours of the morning, by the time we had pushed and shoved our way through the shoulder to shoulder crowds from the Opera House back up to Wynyard Station, then managed to squeeze onto a train where we sat on the floor all the way home. And at 3am, in the flickering light of candles on our balcony, is where we threw back quite a few strawberry champagne cocktails to toast in the New Year — in the peace and serenity of the early morning, tucking into cold smoked salmon and a delicious plate of pate du fois. To this day it's a deep, dark secret how one obtains a security pass to get into the Opera House to watch the fireworks on New Year's Eve and this information I would never ever divulge. Never. Not in a million years.

A number of weddings were performed on ocean cruise liners but after 9/11 security was tightened considerably and celebrants were no longer allowed to board these ships to marry the happy couple before they sailed off out to through the Heads and into the sunset.

Chapter 7 — *Location, Location, Location*

Shelly Beach at Manly was another favourite venue especially where breasts were concerned, the male guests often being provided with the 'female delight' on a Saturday or Sunday afternoon. Many sunbathed topless, so it wasn't unusual for me to perform a ceremony with the men staring at a beach bosom beauty instead of the bride. At least the beach bosom beauty had hers uncovered. My mother was staying with us one time, so came along to watch the 'wedding spectacular' which didn't disappoint from a topless point of view.

I hadn't noticed a group of topless young things provocatively baring their breasts until I heard Mother loudly ask for all the guests to hear, 'Darling, who are those women with their bosoms hanging out like watermelons?'

I saw them but too late, and not before my elderly mother marched over to them and ordered them to 'get dressed because there's a wedding about to begin or else I'll report you.'

It went without saying she was an old school mistress and it never, ever really wore off.

Mollymook is a gem of a place on the South Coast, another world almost, another lifetime and, 'Yes, I'd be delighted to go down to Mollymook' I told the Mother of the Bride on the phone, a sea-change location is just what the doctor ordered.

But this was the peak of Summer and already the bush fires had started down the South Coast and approaching the area, great gusts of flames were spreading across the road and we were lucky to get through.

Hectares were destroyed that year and the smouldering countryside spelt the dreadful tale. Having stayed in a motel the night of the wedding, we woke to discover the fires had spread further and it was impossible to return back up the Highway towards Nowra, instead we were diverted south to Batemans Bay, then up through Braidwood and around the back of Lake George through Tarago, north to Goulburn and back to Robertson in the Southern Highlands.

143

The return trip which should have only taken us just over an hour and a half, took nearly six hours with only a quick pit stop in Goulburn.

I could hear the familiar phrase going through my head — I think I'll become a celebrant, it looks a great job. Yeah right, what about the petrol bills and the extra time it takes to get home? And what about working every day of the week, rain, hail or shine with a few bush fires thrown in for good measure?

Of course a brilliant view for photography is important for wedding venues and nothing attracts like the location of the Harbour Bridge. 'And if it rains,' they say, 'we can shelter underneath.'

I can assure all aspiring celebrants, brides and grooms that the Harbour Bridge does not provide shelter; instead it acts as a huge wind tunnel and the rain sweeps through it at top speed, so the bridal veil needs to be very firmly anchored. Just as I was to declare a couple 'husband and wife', a great gust of wind I reckon to have been about twenty knots, literally knocked us off our feet and the bride's veil was suddenly whipped from her head. It instantly billowed out like a huge white parachute, and then without warning, tore itself away from the bride's head in just a matter of seconds. It resembled a scurrying cirrus strata cloud as it went higher and higher before it came down, right out in the middle of Sydney Harbour.

'Oh my veil,' wailed the bride, 'can someone go in and get it?' Go in and get it? I don't know who laughed loudest, myself or the rest of the guests, and as I called for congratulations, the Rivercat zoomed around the edge of Hickson Road Reserve, a Channel Nine helicopter zoomed over the Harbour Bridge and a train passed directly overhead and rumbled its way down into the Wynyard Station tunnel.

All this noise added to the roar of the wind, and never was I more pleased to get inside my car, turn on the heater and drive on to the next wedding, even though I was wet and frozen to the

Chapter 7 — *Location, Location, Location*

bone. And that was *without* swimming out into the harbour to retrieve the bride's veil.

'And what is your occupation?' I asked looking up from the paperwork.

'We aren't in the habit of referring to what we are most professional in, as our "occupation",' snarled Mr Up-Himself, 'we refer to it as our "profession", we're "Super Execs",' he went on to explain, 'just put that down as our *profession*,' he emphasised. 'Super Execs,' he repeated. Yes, I'd heard that one before.

Here was I enjoying the so-called fine company of the Super Execs whilst completing the paperwork — of course nothing was going to go wrong on *their* wedding day, 'we have everything organised, totally organised,' they told me.

'We have secured the services of a wedding planner,' purred Ms Up-Herself-Super-Exec. Of course again, it's location, location, location and nothing could be better that Nielsen Park at Vaucluse, 'because *we* live in Vaucluse,' I was informed. Big bloody deal I thought, wait 'til you experience the smoky barbecues and soccer balls and the dozens of cars and your guests, who can't park anywhere, then have to climb up the path to Greycliffe House in the heat. Not so strange I think sometimes, how things come back to bite you as that afternoon Sydney experienced one of its wildest Summer tropical storms. Striking with the greatest precision as storms do, right in the middle of the ceremony, the heavens opened up and drenched like Balmain Water Rats we all raced down the grassy slope to the little iron roofed shed, where upon the wedding 'a capella' singers opened up in full chorus.

Thinking we had finished the ceremony, they kept on singing and singing but eventually the groom managed to get them to stop so I could declare them husband and wife.

But no-one really heard because the rain on the corrugated iron roof drowned me out and most guests had gone straight to the bar anyway.

145

The Big Day

They weren't there to listen to a boring old ceremony; alcohol was a more attractive option to a hot and drenched guest.

Especially as the bride and groom lived in Vaucluse and seemingly, money was obviously no object. So much for nothing going wrong on *their* Big Day.

Shelly Beach at Manly was also another washout. The bride was running late but had she turned up at the appointed hour then this would have been a near perfect wedding location.

As the storm clouds gathered overhead and the readings dragged on and on about 'love and cherish, respect and caring', large splats of rain started to come down. But it didn't matter to beautiful Sophie who insisted we carry on with the ceremony.

My roadie took off with the briefcase and paperwork while the violinists ran for cover but there was no stopping Sophie who hissed, 'Carry on Wendy, I've just *got* to get married on the beach.' Never, ever will I do another beach wedding because if the rain doesn't get you, then the sunstroke will, right on the back of the neck because that's where you have to stand for a whole hour in the mid-day sun, waiting for the bride, while your poor skin frazzles and fries itself to death. Or you get drenched like a drowned rat because of the couple's dream of getting married on the beach. No-one cares if you end up feeling sick and dizzy on a Saturday night with the prospect of another couple of weddings to do the next day, or if you've just got pneumonia from the freezing wind and rain when you're soaked to death because *she's* the bride and despite having been appointed by the Federal Attorney General, *you're* only just the celebrant and that's just the way it is.

* * *

'Wendy, mind if we get married at your place?' asked the Lovely Leanne.

'Of course not,' I replied, 'it'll be much easier for you than having to find a venue in the middle of Winter.'

Chapter 7 — *Location, Location, Location*

The Lovely Leanne's Big Day arrived and the buzzer sounded from the intercom.

'Come on up, Leanne,' I called.

Opening my apartment door into the hallway, there stood the Lovely Leanne in the largest marquee of all times but it was truly beautiful to say the least.

'Leanne you look gorgeous, come on in everyone,' I said.

But the Lovely Leanne couldn't fit through my front door. She twisted the hoop in the dress this way and twisted it that way. She raised her skirts and bent forward but still the Lovely Leanne couldn't fit through the door.

'Bloody hell,' exclaimed the Lovely Leanne, 'there's only one answer to all this,' and with that, she turned her back to me and said, 'unzip me Wendy, and I'll take the damned thing off.' Leaving the huge hooped dress out in the hallway Leanne strode in to the middle of my lounge room, decked out in her white wedding lingerie, while we carried the dress sideways through the door and into the middle of the floor, whereupon the Lovely Leanne clambered back into the middle of the hoop, dragged the rest of the dress up, carefully manoeuvred her breasts back into the bodice, re-zipped it and we got on with the wedding. But not until we had moved the lounge suite sideways and the coffee table out onto the balcony was there enough room for the bride and groom to stand side-by-side, together with their fifteen guests and a guest's video tripod just thrown in for good measure.

147

Chapter 8
Stir Fry

All day little yellow envelopes would jump into my Inbox.

'My son Yasir is M.A. English looking for his match at Australia from Delhi. Spouse is needed honest, fine and beautiful.'

The internet attracted heaps of unusual requests as many overseas people thought I was the Match-Maker made in heaven.

From Dumb Dumb Darlas to Delhi — many thought my website was an Introduction Agency. Some requests were plain sad.

Dear Miss Wendy
I look on the internet and find your business name Wendy Bull, Sydney City Celebrant because I seek girl to marry and move to Australia.

I am university graduate from Delhi in business and I need pretty attractive Australian girl to make my life happy and start a new life with babies.

I am a keen student who wishes to live in Australia so I beg you to help me to find a beautiful girl to marry. I beg you please Miss Wendy.

I can be found on this email return.

And yet another:

Hello dear!
Hello and how are you doing, dear? I hope you are fine with family and friends too. I am in need of love; also seeking for someone that I can call my own. I know this will sound as a surprise to you since we haven't communicate before now or don't even know each other at the moment but I also know that the journey of a thousand mile must start with a step that is why I want to know more about you and also I will like to let you know more about me to and even to give you entrance into my life, I mean, I need a serious and real relationship, not just a mail friend or pen pals or phone or chatting friends, I need a someone who will be ready for both of us to meet each other face to face, I need someone that I can see and talk with face to face, if you are also interested kindly write back for us to talk and know each other more better, I will be waiting to read from you, take care of yourself and may God be with you.
Your friend to be.

They kept coming:

Dear Wendy Miss
Please can you organise a bridal car and a bridal dress for my wife to be. We are coming from Bangladesh and I want our special day to become perfect. When is the best time to arrive in Australia?

I still don't know who they are and they never booked me for their wedding. For obvious reasons, brides and grooms were found on the internet as this was hugely time saving and it also saves a bloke sitting in a bar for hours on end waiting for a hopeful 'bottle girl' to turn up. But what often turns up at the airport, after countless emails in which the corresponding couple have declared their love for each other, isn't always as expected. Anna turned up as prepared as any eager bride could be, with her trousseau packed into four huge suitcases but Ken wasn't at all impressed — the ugly Anna had been sending photos of her pretty and much younger, 'drop dead gorgeous' sister Sophia-Maria, a much more attractive and much thinner variety than the poor little squat and pudgy Anna. For whatever reason, Ken felt somewhat obliged to go through with the marriage but it lasted exactly three months, as Anna hated cooking and housework; in fact she hated work of any description.

Ken confided that she lay in bed reading all morning and in the afternoons watched 'Oprah', 'Dr Phil' and 'The Bold and the Beautiful'.

He'd come home to a house that looked like a pigsty, with the ever-increasing, bulging Anna insisting they go to restaurants for dinner 'to save her cooking.' But Ken seriously doubted she could do that anyway. But as luck would have it for Ken, he didn't get her pregnant and the Immigration Department refused Anna's application for a Spouse Visa and had taken a dim view of her marrying as she had only arrived on a Tourist Visa. Thus the blushing bride was sent packing right back to where she came from, much to Ken's great relief. Ken arrived on my doorstep the following afternoon with a bottle of champagne.

'The divorce will be the easy part, compared to having the ugly, fat Anna as a wife,' he confided to me, finishing off the entire bottle on his own.

Many couples had never so much as held hands before they met at 'Arrivals' at Mascot airport but had built their relationship through emails and phone calls; however, I often wondered about tolerance of unknown personal habits such as body odour, halitosis due to lack of oral hygiene and not wearing deodorant, as some were not aware these things were mandatory to most Australians and weren't generally discussed in their emails as a pre-requisite to marriage.

In the space of thirteen years Jonathan married three internet brides, who all bore him children in quick succession but left

The Big Day

him after the delights of marriage wore thin. The ex-brides and all their children lived happily ever after in the good, old, kind and lucky country called Australia where, despite people like Jonathan paying a pile of alimony, the government hands out the handfuls of cash every fortnight and offers everyone a wonderful future with opportunities, compared to where they were born, and where they would have otherwise have spent a lifetime of misery plucking chooks in the family's backyard or sitting behind an old singer sewing machine in some far-off factory earning twenty cents a day. The 'Lucky Country'. So many saw it as their big and bright future, where the country looked after you, providing you made every attempt at turning up for a job interviews seeking employment and didn't break the law.

Sometimes it worked well if the relationship with the new spouse was honest and successful. Unfortunately that was really only a matter of luck as it was impossible for couples to really learn to know each other before marriage.

* * *

Trying to extend her visa, and thinking marriage was a good idea, I had Mai on the phone.

'How soon can we get married?' she asked.

'One calendar month,' I explained. 'That means one month and one day after you come and sign the Notice of Intended Marriage.'

'Not good enough!' snapped Mai, 'I want to get married next weekend.'

'Why so soon?' I asked her.

'My visa expire and I must get married quick.'

'Impossible. Sorry, Mai,' I told her, 'just because you get married here to an Australian it doesn't mean you are allowed to stay in the country.'

Chapter 8 — *Stir Fry*

'Don't worry,' she confessed. 'I find other way to stay, quite easy; have friend with sewing business in garage. No-one know I here anyway, even when my passport expire. Just use other name, and use friend's passport. We look the same. No-one know.'

And the phone went dead.

*　*　*

There was always the 'unusual' on The Big Day which made life so much more interesting and generally brought a smile to my lips. Totally famished at 2 pm one Saturday afternoon in between weddings, we stopped at a club for a cooling respite — a cold drink and something to eat. As I was tucking into a salad I noticed a table of Egyptians who were all craning around to look at me. Politely smiling but with a full mouth, I gave them a slight smile, a nod and then continued to finish my lunch.

As we were leaving after our hurried stop and passed their table, a young woman smiling broadly, jumped up and grabbed my arm.

'Wendy, Wendy, you remember me; I was in one of your classes at TAFE. You teach me marketing.' So as not to appear rude and having forgotten her name, I said, 'Of course I remember you; how are you?'

Dressed in a black suit, wearing my celebrant's name badge and carrying my briefcase, I suppose I did look on the formal side of things. Hebatella kept hold of my arm, and turned to her family. Waving her arms and speaking loudly and quickly in Arabic, she told them who I was and the likely, 'rank and status'. Suddenly the whole table rose to their feet and lots of very enthusiastic bowing started to take place upon which they all began crossing themselves as for a divine blessing.

Hebatella feeling proud to have discovered me, kept them at it, obviously telling them to keep going. The more bowing that went on, the more they genuflected with great fervour and the

153

more uncomfortable I became. By this time they had created quite a lot of attention from the other club patrons and a hush came over the whole room.

But enough was enough, so I had to raise my hand and ask them all to 'please stop'. So Hebatella then explained to me: 'I told them you were a highly appointed person, like our Egyptian Coptic Orthodox priests; you can marry people, so they must acknowledge your status and ask for your blessing.' After shaking hands with all the family, and saying 'Bless you' to everyone three times, I politely excused myself as Hebatella followed me out to the car and promised to keep in touch. Bless dear Hebatella but I never heard from her again; however, in some sense, I felt strangely honoured that day, for sure.

* * *

It was generally a delight to officiate at marriages of those from mixed nationalities. Couples always seemed so much more grateful and they would shake my hand urgently and, little old ladies not understanding any English would bury their emotional, crying faces into my chest, and leave an array of Elizabeth Arden colours across the front of my suit. Of course there were terribly sad weddings when families would not accept their future daughter or son-in-law because they weren't of the same nationality or religion and would boycott the whole proceedings. Lie Hiong and Sam were one such couple. Sam came from a devout Greek family who would not accept his Asian bride under any circumstances and only one aunt turned up at the wedding making it quite clear to Sam that 'I'm here only to represent the family.' No-one in Sam's family approved of the marriage. Lie Hiong's close family, seventeen in all, had all made the trip from Shanghai: her parents, brothers and sisters and all their children, including the most gorgeous one-year-old identical twin boys.

Lie Hiong's father stood tall and proud beside his daughter. Everyone cried, even Sam, for his 'lost' family who would not attend. But my day was otherwise brightened when I asked Lie Hiong's Mandarin speaking father, 'Who brings this bride to be married?'

Lie Hiong had taught him to say, 'I do' in English for when she gave him the nod but I suspected he knew more English than he was letting on, as he answered right on cue.

And as he spoke he bowed to me and, looking up with a happy face, he replied, '*I do!* Yes, *I do*, *I do*, yes, I *do* … and yes *I do* love Opera House and *I do* love Harbour Bridge, velly, velly much. I *do!*' Lie Hiong and Sam sent Christmas cards for many years until we somehow both lost touch after we moved from Balmain.

* * *

I married hundreds of couples from around the globe but never any who were as pedantic as the Dutch couple, Hans and Maja. Hans and Maja had their push bikes flown from Schipol Amsterdam to Cairns, where they explored North Queensland from Cape York in the north, across into the west of the Atherton Tablelands and then headed south, pedalling in true energetic Dutch style as they went.

From the Daintree to Darlinghurst, they rode their bikes down the long stretch of the Pacific Highway to Sydney, where they were to marry, before they pushed on down to Melbourne. There they would have the great dismantle again before the bikes would be loaded onto a Jetstar and off over to Tasmania. After arriving in Sydney, Hans and Maja came to meet me, declaring Australia to be, 'One very big country, much bigger than the Netherlands, and so very far to bike. Lots of very long roads.'

Of course I knew this, having driven myself many times from Cairns to Sydney but certainly not on a push bike. Leave the

The Big Day

cycling madness to the Dutch! Hans and Maja asked me with serious faces, 'Could vee please get married viz our bikes?'

'Of course', I told them, 'whatever you want.' So, Hans and Maja arrived at the Royal Botanic Gardens with their bikes, dressed in full cycling regalia which included their trusty, cycling helmets.

A very short but solemn ceremony followed with Warren the photographer clicking away trying to get romantic and meaningful pics — even 'the kiss' was exchanged with Hans and Maja firmly holding on to their handle bars. Warren called next day. 'Wendy, it was dreadful,' he said, 'they wouldn't let go of their handle bars; they absolutely forced me — every shot had to have the bikes in. Bikes with the Opera House, bikes on the Harbour Bridge, bikes with the harbour, bikes with the city skyline, bikes with the statues, bikes by the pond and bikes with the flowers. I couldn't prise them away from their bloody bikes; they clutched them like mad. I could hardly get any romantic shots.'

'Well Warren,' I comforted him, saying, 'if that's what they wanted, then that's what they got. You did as you were asked and that's it.' Several weeks later I received an email from Den Haag in The Netherlands which read:

Dear Wendy

Hello. This is Hans here. We enjoyed our bike trip in Australia and getting married, although Australia is much bigger than the Netherlands. You were a very good celebrant and helpful, thank you. It is a long way. But Maja and I have received Warren's photos and we are very disappointed because there are no romantic photos, just us and our bikes.

Please can you explain this for us? I hope you visit us in Den Haag when you come.

Best wishes

Hans.

So I wrote back:

Dear Hans and Maja

It was lovely hearing from you and pleased to hear that you are both safe and well, back in Den Haag. I have spoken to Warren about the photos, but he tells me he asked you many times to have photographs without your bikes, so he could take some lovely romantic pictures of you both with the Opera House and Harbour Bridge as a backdrop but you both wanted to have your bikes in all of the pictures; therefore he was unable to take proper wedding photography. He did as you asked and complied with your wishes — I am very sorry you did not let him take correct wedding photography in which he is highly professional. I hope to visit you in The Netherlands one day and look forward to meeting you again.

Very best wishes,
Wendy.

But I didn't go and see them when I went to the Netherlands a year or so later. I thought it best to let sleeping dogs lie.

So that was the end of that. Surely the bikes could have been left out of *some* photos — but no, they had been adamant. So many photographers are given very strict briefs from couples about what they want and leave the photographer no option but to bow to their demands. The complaints later on would just have to fall on deaf ears.

* * *

I learned to suggest to Asian brides to have their photographs taken after their tea ceremony and prior to the marriage ceremony so they would have plenty of time in the day for socialising.

Often I would ask them to invite their guests half an hour early and in some cases, even an hour before the ceremony was to begin, so that not only could we start on time but also it would ensure that all the guests would be there when the ceremony commenced.

Asian brides were invariably late, due to several dress changes and travelling to various places across Sydney for extra photos prior to the ceremony, so I discovered this was indeed good practice. Some thought they could book me for the whole day and I would just sit there waiting for them, whatever time they turned up.

I reminded many couples that celebrants were like doctors: appointments are appointments — and other couples required my services.

Often though, it made no difference what I said.

* * *

Beginning 40 minutes *after* the appointed starting time in Balmain, the ceremony went without a hitch — a gorgeous bride and her very good-looking groom. Smiling, talking and clapping throughout the service were the norm. It was a beautiful ceremony and both fathers were invited to be the witnesses taking their job very seriously. After shaking hands and eventually leaving their home, I was putting my briefcase, amplifier and signing lectern back into the car when a couple came racing across the road towards me. 'Are you the celebrant?' asked the man breathlessly.

After assuring him I was, he asked, 'Where are you going?'

'Off to my next wedding,' I replied.

'But you can't,' insisted the man. 'We haven't seen the bride and groom get married.'

'Sorry,' I said, 'we were scheduled for 2 o'clock and we even started late as it was, and it's now nearly 4 o'clock. I've got to go and do my next wedding, so if you'll excuse me … '

But the couple stood there with mouths wide open, 'But we didn't see them get married,' cried the girl as I crossed the road towards my car. 'Can't you just come back and do it again?'

Chapter 8 — *Stir Fry*

'Again?' I thought. 'Again?' That'll be the day.

* * *

The many times I have encountered people who run in to the ceremony over an hour late, never surprises me. It was just plain lack of respect for the bride and groom who had gone to every effort to organise their special day.

And it was also very, very rude — just plain rude. Jen came up with a good one.

She sent an account to all the couples who hadn't turned up on her Big Day but had said they were definitely attending.

'I had to fork out for them, so they can bloody well pay me back,' she told me on the phone after she returned home from her honeymoon.

We didn't contact each other again so I don't know how many people reimbursed her. But good try, Jen. I love your style.

* * *

There are some fabulous and very romantic weddings, fairy lights and candles, romantic music and well-heeled guests, in the most beautiful of settings.

There are intimate hotel suite liaisons with discreet waiters in black hovering in the shadows, brides looking as glam as the covers of Vogue, champagne flutes, strawberries, caviar, quail and smoked salmon. The full catastrophe.

Ah! But the Italian: Count Valentino, as the name suggests, was tall, dark and handsome and never have I encountered such manners. Certainly they were one of the loveliest couples, amongst many that I had the pleasure of meeting. His accent said it all and Valentino always comes to mind not only for total perfection of the well-organised and immaculately attired wedding but also for his name. Aptly named, aptly behaved and

The Big Day

aptly titled. I wish all my couples were like Valentino and his beautiful well-mannered bride.

* * *

One year I had a real run of Russian brides who were always very demanding and changed their wedding plans as often as their husbands drank vodka. One demanding Russian couple changed their ceremony venue five times and on the day assured me that they could get married on the lawns of Government House.

I have never had approval for a Government House wedding. I told them it wasn't allowed.

But I was told in broken English, not to worry — we were to meet at Government House gates at the appointed time, 'I am a Doctor; zay vill let uz in.'

As the couple thought they knew someone on the 'inside', so to speak, the bridal car arrived, pulling up at the gates, 40 minutes late. The groom shot out, demanding that the gate person let us through.

As expected, the security person would not unlock the heavy wrought iron gates, and informed them in no uncertain manner that they were definitely not allowed to have the ceremony on the lawn. Fortunately, they demurely settled for the lawns next door in the Royal Botanic Gardens instead. Even then they couldn't make their minds up exactly where on the lawn they wanted to stand — and with black clouds looming closer overhead, I took control and insisted they stand with Government House behind them so they could pretend they were in the grounds. This seemed to satisfy them and on with the ceremony I went, just as the rain started to fall on the marriage register.

* * *

One Thai bride arrived at my office with take-away Thai for my dinner as I had expressed my liking for Thai food over the phone when we'd been chatting prior to meeting and I also had a beautiful Turkish couple arrive with a huge box of Turkish Delights. Such treats, and they came often! An Egyptian couple arrived bearing Egyptian marzipan and the English came bearing gifts of English toffee and boiled sweets. One couple arrived with Earl Grey tea and Scottish shortbreads which we all enjoyed together as we finalised the paperwork. I even received an enchanting little thimble souvenir from a couple who sailed the world on the Queen Mary to marry here in Sydney. Chocolates, flowers and bottles of wine all arrived on my doorstep from appreciative couples. I have many boxes of thank you cards and letters, and fifteen folders of emails of appreciation I could never bear to throw away.

Buddhists often come to my home to get married and we all light incense and candles, and pray together in front of my little brass Chinese Buddha in the hallway.

The four great qualities of Loving Kindness, Compassion, Joy (in the joy of others) and Equanimity (calmness in mood or temper) are foremost in their ceremonies.

I am generally left with the traditional Buddhist food offerings, oranges and apples being the main speciality, but occasionally I end up with bunches of bananas or grapes, and once I was left with a big fat green custard apple and a nice big juicy but very prickly pineapple.

The Falun Dafa also often arrive on my doorstep declaring truthfulness, compassion and forbearance. Their ceremonies are comprised of the virtues of their way of life, increasing wisdom and improving morality, which in turn, teaches one to look inside oneself and seek spiritual growth and enlightenment.

They also quote Mr Li Hongzhi's teachings about the values of virtue, happiness and personal further advancement.

The Big Day

Branching away from the day to day traditional type ceremonies, the Buddhist and Falun Dafa (or Falun Gong) are an absolute delight and certainly a welcome change to the 'ordinary type' ceremony.

I perform many an Asian wedding because I was am considered the 'Lucky Celebrant' because of the number eight which appears often in my contact details. Asian clients will discover I have the number eight in my street address, my office telephone and also my fax number, in my Celebrant number, Justice of the Peace number, Post Office Box number and unbeknown to them, I was allocated a number eight in my on-line number with Births Deaths and Marriages. Good old number eight — it brought me many Asian weddings, especially as I live in Chatswood.

Many Russians, however, can be a true delight, especially a group of nine Russian men who had all ended up marrying lovely Japanese girls. Arriving at the humble abode of yet another Russian man and his Japanese bride-to-be, I encountered the same warm hospitality as previously offered.

Whilst the little Japanese ladies shuffled around in the kitchen icing cakes and preparing food, the men relaxed in the lounge room, tossing back unmeasured amounts of vodka to celebrate the future marital bliss of yet another comrade. Eventually we started the ceremony in their tiny lounge, with Boris and Umi holding hands and gazing at each other in the most delightful way.

But after I declared them 'husband and wife' Boris did not kiss his bride but instead raised his hand in true military style and asked everyone to stop clapping whilst he launched into a vodka-induced speech entirely in Russian. The young Japanese ladies and I waited patiently as Boris' speech went on and on, stopping five times, while the guests' glasses were refilled with vodka, then finally, glasses raised, they all toasted each other, tossing it back while Boris continued on with the speech.

Chapter 8 — *Stir Fry*

The little Japanese ladies and I were still in complete silence. Finally, the inebriated Russians stopped and Boris turned towards me and said loudly in English.

'Thank you Wendy, you are very good celebrant and we salute you. In my speech I make apology to Russian Government — my motherland, that I do not marry Russian bride, but instead I marry pretty Japanese lady and very good cook, Japanese girl called Umi. Motherland I am sorry!' With that, Boris, tanked to the eyeballs from a full bottle of vodka erupted into a flood of tears and sobbed his heart out (I suppose) for his motherland. The little Japanese ladies, with the bride in tow, not knowing what to do next, quietly filed back into the kitchen to finish preparing the food.

* * *

The hospitality of many non-Australians certainly outshone the 'would-be's if they could be'. Early one morning in a thick pea-soup fog, I left the Southern Highlands to travel up to the northern beaches of Sydney to Palm Beach to perform a ceremony. It's a long journey up the M5 to Sydney and back again without as much as a glass of water.

Arriving back in the Southern Highlands in the afternoon, I pulled up in the drive of a beautiful country home where I was booked to perform my next ceremony. As I rang the bell, Elizabeth, 'Mrs Bucket, the Lady of the House' (as I came to call her), appeared with a withering smile.

Upon entering the wide reception area I asked quietly if I could please have a glass of water before I commenced her son's ceremony, as I had just completed a long journey — up to Sydney and back.

'Mrs Bucket — The Lady of the House' frowned at my request and announced, 'Not at all possible I'm afraid, the maid has just finished tidying the kitchen and we mustn't dirty the glasses for the toasts.'

The Big Day

'Oh dear,' I replied, 'well perhaps you could show me the ladies' powder room.'

'That's impossible too,' she continued. 'It's all ready and clean for the guests but you can use the maids' loo downstairs near the scullery, *if you must*.' Briefcase and all I tripped down a winding set of back stairs to the maids' toilet room and thankfully used the maids' loo. Swishing water into my hands from the tap over the basin I had a lovely cool drink, repaired my makeup and reappeared at the top of the stairs.

'Ready now?' sniped 'Mrs Bucket — The Lady of the House' as she strode ahead of me out onto the side lawn where the ceremony was to be held. The groom, whose mother Elizabeth, was indeed 'Mrs Bucket — The Lady of the House', looked smart but nervous, and the bride arriving all of 50 minutes late, looked lovely and was full of apologies for her overdue arrival. But 'Mrs Bucket — The Lady of the House' did not endear herself to me. So having been treated like the local char, which was not uncommon from these would-be's, I shook hands with the guests and left as quietly as I had come.

I have lost count of the number of times I was tempted to do wheelies in their gravel driveways and certainly encountered my share of 'Mrs Buckets' in the Southern Highlands.

* * *

But the hospitality of the real country folk was enormous and many a time I was urged to stay on for the party or barbecue, most of which I generally declined simply because there was always 'the trip home', the fog and the real threat of a wallaby or kangaroo hopping out onto the road and meeting the front of my car with a deadly bump just as the sun went down. Had I stayed on and consumed a few glasses of red, it wouldn't have been such a good idea.

Chapter 8 — *Stir Fry*

Burradoo in the Southern Highlands is a suburb of Bowral and it was here I had been asked to go and discuss wedding plans for some upcoming nuptials. I couldn't place the accent at first but the woman sounded South American and indeed upon meeting, I discovered she was.

After pressing the security buttons at the front gate, which allowed the gates to slowly open to let me enter, I drove inside and up the gravel drive to the house.

Such a warm welcome and certainly no 'would be' host; instead I was invited to perch up at the kitchen bar, where out came the glasses and a bottle of red, and a plate of freshly plated nachos.

At 11 o'clock in the morning this wasn't my usual drink but deciding to graciously accept the generous spirit of South American hospitality, I sipped as I got on with the paperwork. It had to be twelve o'clock somewhere in the world, I thought. 'Is your fiancé here?' I asked after Carla had signed the Notice of Intended Marriage. 'I need him to sign the paperwork, as well.'

'He upstairs asleep,' was the reply.

'I really need him to sign this,' I said, so Carla grabbed her mobile phone and called upstairs to the groom.

After I had waited patiently for about half an hour and with another glass of red in my hand, Leon came sauntering down the spiral staircase, wrapping himself in a white bathrobe.

After introductions and a brief conversation, and with the paperwork completed, he turned to me and said, 'Everything is very good; now we get married next month. Carla pay you the money. Goodbye.' With that, Carla moved over to a kitchen cupboard and asked, 'How much you charge?'

'$550,' I said almost apologetically, 'and that includes GST.'

With that Carla swung around to face me, saying, '$550? That all?'

'Yes, $550 is what I charge for local weddings,' I replied.

With that, Carla reached down into a cupboard below the kitchen sink and brought out a wine-sized cardboard box and flipping up the top folders, revealed what must have been hundreds of thousands of dollars all stacked neatly into tidy piles.

'Come on,' she said. 'I give you more than $550; plenty more money here; you take more money.'

'No,' I insisted, 'only $550, thanks Carla.'

Carla slowly peeled off $550 and slowly put the cardboard box back down inside the cupboard.

'OK,' she said, 'on day of wedding, you stay for dinner.'

'Thank you Carla,' I said, 'but I have another wedding to go to after yours so can't possibly stay, sorry, but I thank you all the same for your very kind invitation.' The day of wedding was lovely and arriving through the gates I noticed just one other car parked on the gravel.

'Where are all your guests?' I asked Carla at the front door.

'Oh Wendy, no-one want to come,' she replied looking sad.

'Never mind,' I said brightly, 'you look such a lovely bride, Carla.' As we moved through the house I noticed its perfect interior design, with thick expensive five metre curtains which hung from ceiling to floor and the wonderful antique bookshelves and cabinets that graced every room.

It was all simply perfectly designed, furnished and decorated from top to toe. The dining table which seated 24 was set with the most exquisite chinaware, silver cutlery and tall stemmed crystal glasses. It was a rather sad scenario though, with the four only guests and the caterers who quietly worked in the gourmet-designed kitchen preparing the delicious luncheon which was to follow and I rather wish I could have accepted Carla's invitation to stay.

*** * * ***

Chapter 8 — *Stir Fry*

Burradoo is supposedly built over (or is it beside?) the local sewerage treatment works, or poo-plant as we called it. Although many chose to ignore this dreadful association, many chose to highlight its unfortunate closeness.

Search as I might, I could never find the meaning of the Aboriginal name 'Burradoo' so I nicknamed it 'Burrapoo', despite the reasonable elegance of the homes which were built upon its smelly foundations.

The local Wingecarribee Shire Council seemed to always keep a fairly low profile on this one, as did the residents. I think they had a lot to answer for. I invented the names 'Burra-do' and 'Burra-don't'. The 'do's' have old money and manners and the 'don'ts' have neither.

It was usually the 'don'ts' who lived there and who found it sooo hard to let the Marriage Celebrant use the maids' quarters so she could have a well-deserved pee after a day out on the road.

Burrawang, also in the Southern Highlands, I nick-named 'Burra-wank' because many of the weekenders were up themselves and came down at the weekend to live in their 'weekenders'. These 'country retreats', as they are advertised in the local real estate pages, are usually old weatherboard structures built in the 30s and 40s or maybe even earlier. Burrawang has become popular because of the quaint village feel and the glorious old pub which serves as the watering hole. Real estate agents have pushed up the prices, which meant that house buyers end up paying exorbitant prices for crappy, run-down old shacks. Therefore Burrawang became 'Burra-wank' and thus made it more of a 'wank' than it really is — although I must admit that a couple of the local families were some of the nicest one could ever meet and we remain friends to this day.

The couple who had the second shortest wedding were locals who lived in Burrawang. The husband called me two weeks after the ceremony to ask if I had processed the paperwork because he suddenly realised he'd made a dreadful mistake.

The Big Day

'She's just a thorough bitch; does fuck-all around the house and is pissed by the time she's supposed to cook some tea,' the nutter whined to me. 'But too late, she cried' as the saying goes; he was married, like it or not.

The Aboriginal name 'Burrawang' means 'nut tree' so I wasn't far wrong about most of the people who went to live there. Most of the locals were great but please spare me from having to marry the nutty, weekend, yuppie element, who wore their jumpers around their shoulders with their shirt collars turned up.

The locals called them 'blow-ins' and laughed at them behind their backs.

* * *

Bong Bong Racecourse in the Highlands attracted quite a few weddings, either because the couple met at the annual Bong Bong race meeting or they just liked the sound of the name.

We never let on a ceremony was to take place there — we just turned up and 'did it' as many would say. An Aboriginal elder from the Tharawal tribe, which came from around the Southern Highlands area, told me that 'bong' meant 'bottom' so the naming of Bong Bong probably came from 'bung bung' meaning buttocks.

'Bong' or 'bung' also meant 'death' in another Aboriginal tribal language.

But as there are about 250 Aboriginal languages across 7,800 tribes, sometimes an exact meaning was a bit hard to find. But I combined the two meanings and nicknamed the Bong Bong Race Track 'Dead Bums' much to the horror of anyone around the Highlands, whom I ever decided to tell.

* * *

Chapter 8 — *Stir Fry*

The shortest marriage only lasted three days, from Thursday afternoon until Sunday morning when the bride confessed to her Indian mother she had tied the knot with her unemployed and inexperienced 21-year-old boyfriend of one year.

He was only here on a tourist visa, had no income and thought if he married here in Australia he could stay as a permanent resident.

Despite Immigration warning him that he had to return home when his visa expired, he did not heed the warning.

The bride's mother was far from impressed when told about the wedding but I was after all, only doing my job.

'Wendy,' Usha whined on the phone. 'I make very bad choice. He's a useless husband in bed, has no proper idea what to do and anyway, he doesn't even like the way my mother cooks our Indian curry. Can you throw away the paperwork?'

'Sorry Usha,' I informed her, 'the paperwork cannot be thrown away under any circumstances.' It always pays to give a lot of thought to the sanctity of marriage.

* * *

Young or old, I enjoyed marrying them as beautifully and sincerely as possible. To this day the youngest I married off was 18 and the eldest 85, and the most times married anyone admitted to was five times in all. These were all some of the loveliest couples in the world and all still my record holders to this day!

* * *

Then one day, arriving for his appointment, Little Italian Luigi, standing all of about 1.35 metres, with his hands in his pockets and his back straight, knocked on my door. He definitely aspired well to the 'short-man's syndrome'. His gorgeous bride-to-be with breasts as large as over-ripe melons stood beside him, an adorable tall and attractive Brazilian girl who he declared, 'would do the bookwork and wages for my business because I divorce my wife, because she no-use to me anymore because she hate sex and because she's a lazy spoilt bitch anyway. I been far too good to her. Anyway Wendy,' he continued, 'you laugh at this one — the ex-wife she also come to the wedding; she insist if all my five children want to come, then she come as well. So, I invite my five children but they can only come if the lazy old bitch comes too. They all too scared of being left out of the new will. Ha, ha, ha,' laughed Little Luigi loudly, as he bounced up and down on the chair with a definite twinkle in his eye.

So one lovely Saturday afternoon, there was Little Luigi at the altar marrying his beautiful bride with his ex-wife and all five children in tow and his beautiful buxom and breasty Brazilian bride eager to experience a weekend of solid marital sex, and then leave for the office first thing Monday morning to start the bookwork and the wages. God bless Little Luigi. How I wish there'd been more of them on my journeys.

Chapter 9
Names

From Luigi to Longbottom, names often said it all.

'Longbottom?' I asked, thankful I wasn't skyping. 'This line's bad — I'll call you on your landline.'

With just enough time to recompose myself, I picked up the phone again and continued the conversation with Lucy Longbottom.

It reminded me of the bride who had been stuck with 'Sidebottom' all her life, '… and if I hear that bloody awful name ever again after I'm married,' she confided in me when we met, 'I'll jump off the bloody bridge.'

Sometimes it was hard trying to keep a straight face when it came to names.

* * *

Margot told she wanted a short ceremony. 'Just enough for the legals and to do a bit more,' she said. 'I want you to get the damned thing over and done with.'

Margot told me I had to hurry things along, on the day: 'If all the guests haven't turned up on time we'll just start anyway.'

It wasn't difficult to understand why she wanted to get married quickly.

Signing the paperwork after the ceremony, the new Mrs Montgomery looked up and asked, 'When can I start signing my husband's name?'

The Big Day

Getting rid of her maiden name was top priority and I completely understood why.

Grabbing my pen to sign the marriage register, she looked up and stared hard at her father sitting in the front row and then very loudly addressing the guests as she started to sign, called out, 'Thank Christ this will be the last fucking time I sign as a fucking Maggot.'

Poor Margot Maggot, such an indignity having to put up with Maggot for twenty-three long years.

'Mrs Margot Montgomery' had a much better ring to it and I quietly had to agree.

2005 must have been my year for names, as just before Christmas after Margot had rid herself of being a Maggot, Mr Quickly-Come arrived with his bride-to-be.

'I make very good husband,' announced Kien Kim Chan. 'I born in Cho Lon, Vietnam. I got very good job but you get me quickly married, Miss Wendy,' he begged.

'What's the hurry?' I asked.

'Lulu pregnant. She have baby soon,' he announced. Then a puzzled look came over his face as he continued. 'Doctor tell me, I should call myself "Mr Quickly-Come". Then doctor laugh. He say that good name for me. So I tell people to call me Mr Quickly-Come because doctor say good name. But I don't know what he mean, Miss Wendy. You tell me.'

Without replying, I just told him not to worry about it but it was 'always best to call himself Mr Chan' as it stated on his passport.

* * *

Not long afterwards Peter Crapp arrived on my doorstep one cold Winter's morning. 'Nice to meet you, I'm Crapp,' he snapped as he walked past me into my office. Hard to reply to that one, I thought, so I just said, 'Hello Peter, I'm Bull.'

I thought he was going to explode but I think I caught a wry smile on his lips.

Why Peter Crapp hadn't ever legally changed his name I don't know or at best, had simply changed the spelling. This would have alleviated the embarrassment he'd experienced over the years. Had it been my name, I would have even changed it to Crepe — far better than Crapp any day of the week.

*　*　*

Sobb seemed to me to be a 'sad' name to have to put up with all of your life but Simon Sobb, a remarkably nice person, appeared unaffected, despite admitting to loathing it. I suggested it was easy enough for him to change it but he said his father would disinherit him if he ever made mention of it again. I felt incredibly sorry for him, as never had such a pleasant person come to see me about getting married.

*　*　*

The same went for Mr Fagg who confessed he hated Fagg and asked, 'Do I really have to say all my names during the legal vows?'

When I told him all names must be said, a shocked look came over his face. 'But it's Percy Fagg,' he told me with a more horrified look. 'I can't possibly say that in front of Fiona's relatives, people who know me just call me Bruce; it's my middle name. Anyway, Fiona doesn't want to become Mrs Fiona Fagg.'

'Look,' I said, 'go and change it legally if you really hate it that much.' A week later an excited Percy Fagg was on the phone. 'Wendy, I changed it and I've never been happier; for the first time in my life people haven't sniggered at me when they've heard my name.'

173

'So how did you choose a new one?' I asked.

'Well, I went to the White Pages Directory and found something easy that I liked the sound of,' he said, 'so I chose Percy Pinks; it hasn't got any connotations at least and I didn't want to be a boring old Smith or Brown.'

I wasn't sure whether to laugh or cry.

* * *

Richard Shaw hadn't got off lightly either through his life, as he was more commonly called Rick Shaw. Apparently the kids at school had teased him dreadfully, calling him Bamboo Billy especially as he lived in Chatswood.

Something lovely to remember though, was officiating a lovely Renewal of Marriage Vows ceremony for a dear old lady called Rose Hill who actually lived in Rosehill.

* * *

But names, like breasts, became of certain fascination simply because the rare and unexpected were often unveiled, such as the Chinese 'Loo' which I felt mild in comparison to Pooi, Pui and Pong which I encountered many times over. From the very unusual and embarrassing, came the graceful names of Maidens and Swans. Ducks even married Drakes; they seemed to come in pairs like past-life soul-mates.

Still the eclectic mix of names kept coming: I married off Birds and Blackadders, Bulls and Bears, Fishes and Farmers, Kindreds and Loves. In fact I can't make fun of names, as I nearly found myself married to both a Bear and a Drake but somehow, out of all the twists and turns in my life, I ended up marrying a Bull, so I settled for Bull and have used it ever since, even after remarrying.

Bull by name and bull by nature, many have reminded me over the years. Thank heavens for my sense of humour, I've often thought.

Sloshed parents aren't the best to have to cope with at the best of times. Thankfully they didn't present themselves at every wedding but they reared their ugly head more often than not. After yet another lovely ceremony, a morning-suited but very sloshed Father of the Bride staggered towards me. Squinting his eyes and peering closely at my name badge he looked up and said, 'Wendy Bull, eh? Thought you shed Bull.'

'Yes,' I answered, 'and you are?'

'Shimon Partridge,' the round and ruddy faced man spluttered.

'Simon or Shimon?' I asked cheekily.

Simon Partridge burst into volleys of laughter and, still squinting through his alcoholic haze, said in a loud voice in front of the guests, 'Bull Shit, that's yer name. Bull Shit, ha, ha, ha bloody, Bull Shit!' Not being backward in coming forward at the best of times, I replied, 'And so you know why I keep this name of Bull?'

'Ha, ha, ha, bloody Bull Shit more like it!' roared Simon Partridge.

'Well,' I continued, getting up close and personal, 'I keep it so that uneducated people like you, can hopefully spell it without making a mistake.' Simon's round and robust wife dressed in a flowing haze of colours was standing within hearing distance, and so obviously taking full advantage of the situation, said as loudly as she could, 'Good on you Wendy, time someone told him where to get off.'

* * *

But I liked 'Bull'. Tongue in cheek, many a time I would tell a couple I'm Likeabull, or Loveabull, but also very Dependabull or Reliabull.

The Big Day

This old-hat corny silly sort of banter got a bit tiresome but it worked well, on the rare occasion in its appropriate perspective especially when I needed to make my point on some issue or to cover over a faux pas.

As I was born in New Zealand, Maori and Islander names are second nature to me, and having contact with Dutch, Indian and Chinese immigrants and speaking a little French and being of French ancestry, this exposure makes pronunciation relatively easy.

I have never really had much difficulty with Italian names either, Sbisa was as easy as Sbat.

But getting my mouth around some of the Thai names became a bit tricky; names such as Khieopan, Sirapatcharangkul, Jitteethai, Rangkarassamee and Waenkaew.

I also encountered Xaybounheuang and Xayamongkoun, Abdisemedhersi and Onusckevicius-Jacyna

Could you really blame Ngampungpis for wanting to change *her* name? 'Just pronounce it phonetically,' the groom instructed me, 'nam-pung-piss.' Again I tried not to smile.

One gorgeous, and so very polite and demure young Thai bride was called Supaporn — I was told that Supa meant 'first' and Porn translated as 'born'.

I didn't have the heart to suggest she take on an easier Australian name because I knew she'd only ask why and I didn't want to explain how Aussies would interpret the name of Supaporn.

The Attorney General's Department decided in its wisdom we use full names during the ceremony, so after much celebrant discussion it was 'what the boss wanted was what the boss got.'

So with the rain about to shower its blessings on a lovely Thai couple, I was hunched under an umbrella up on Observatory Hill asking a lovely young bride in her faltering English, to repeat after my faltering Thai: 'I call upon those here present, to witness that I, Supaporn Sirapatcharangkul, take you Suriyan Saysanavongphet, to be my wedded husband.' So much easier for me to ask them to say, 'I Sue, take you John, to be my wedded husband' or even 'I, Supaporn, take you Suriyan, to be my wedded husband' and with the legal paperwork correctly completed, and over 50 guests to witness the actual people themselves and who were actually known to the couple, surely the marriage was valid by saying the latter and certainly much less offensive if I had it wrong.

Ah! But this is Australia and one must stick to bureaucratic red tape and rules.

Japanese names such as Takusagawa, Nakatsuka and so on, were relatively easy like the very phonetic Indonesian names; even the Chinese Xiong, Zhao, and Ng were easier than the Thai.

Names seemed to haunt me — or was that because I always dealt with such a wide range of nationalities?

I worked for some time with a finance lending company, with a great mate called Chok Kiat — aka Tony — who told me just prior to the wedding that I would meet his brother who would be one of the witnesses, called Chook Wah but everyone just called him Simon. But I couldn't resist Chook's lovely smile when I was introduced to him, so shaking hands I cheekily said, 'Hi Chook,' much to the delight of the other English-speaking Chinese standing within hearing distance.

Some of my Chinese clients had brilliant and refreshing senses of humour, especially Chok and Chook. I can still see their broad grins.

I encountered many Middle Eastern names such as Ataei Kachouei, Zargarian Sangabarani, Kirakosian Namagerdi, Shirvani Kenaraki and Kasparian Megherdichzadeh, which were often difficult to pronounce during a ceremony. Often they had two family names as opposed to some Indonesians who just had the one name such as Djusni or Dji. I would ask what their first name was but they would insist on just the one name which was a family name and sure enough that's exactly what the passport showed.

And you could sometimes tell the couples who came from 'good' Catholic families, as their fathers' names were Patrick Joseph, Michael Bernard or Aloysius Francis Xavier and they were often married to a Mary Margaret, Mary Therese, Mary Magdalene or a Mary Bernadette, although not necessarily all in that order. Their children were generally named Sara, Angela, Mark, Michael, David, Simon and Thomas. Names spoke volumes! Jewish names were also easy enough to recognise as invariably they were Moses, David, Rebekah, Israel, Abraham, Rachel, Rebecca, Elijah, Samuel and Sarah and so on.

Western Europeans produced some mighty tongue twisters — try pronouncing Kachyckyj or Knezevic after a couple of sherberts down at the pub, or Zarzeczny, Gavrylyuk and Tkaczyk all in that order after a few vodka cocktails at the Melbourne Cup. The Ukrainians didn't disappoint either; Khatuntseva seemed easy in comparison to Talgatovitch or Anatolyevich, especially when you were asking them to repeat all their names during their vows.

I often wondered why we weren't registered with numbers — makes sense, you can't go wrong with numbers. Just imagine how straightforward it would be when saying one's vows: 'I call upon those present to witness that I, 123 take you 567 to be my lawful wedded husband.'

No getting that wrong and I'm surprised that the Australian bureaucracy hasn't already thought of it. We are after all, just numbers to the statisticians in Canberra. So much easier than pronouncing 'Ng' especially when you've done three weddings and your feet are killing you and you've got a blocked nose and your eyes are streaming with the pollen from the trees in the park.

Of course the word 'lawful' often came out as 'awful', especially if the groom had had a few drinks prior to the ceremony, which got the guests laughing with great gusto and often spoilt a very meaningful moment.

Chapter 9 — *Names*

Thankfully celebrants were legally allowed to stop using the word 'lawful' after a few years. Then I'd quietly think of Muriel's Wedding and say to myself, 'You're awful, Muriel' although 'terrible' was the actual word used by Muriel's sister.

But somehow it satisfied my sense of humour.

And neither did those wonderful Hungarians disappoint, as I married off an Angyalffy, a Szekerczes and a Zsigo, but relatively easy I thought, was a Macedonian Stojceski. One beautiful Philippino bride-to-be came up with the best family name rarity of all times — Er-Er.

I could hardly believe Er-Er could be a family name, but Er-Er it was. I thought it was just as well the bride didn't stutter or we'd have never got to the point.

Imagine if both the bride and groom stuttered and both had the same family name of Er-Er it would sound like this:

'I er er Er-Er take you er er Er-Er to be my er er lawful er er wedded er er wife.' An absolute classic — oh such trouble and strife!

But just as I was getting used to the potpourri of migrant names, I was landed with a Gnanathickampillai and after my tongue untangled itself, I launched into the bride's surname which was Jaszczyszyn. Give me Smith, Brown or Bull any day; even Fish, Drake, Duck or Swan; even Burns, Sc or Ng but leave me out of anything even remotely similar to Czesnulewicz.

'And your surname?' I asked the polite gentlemen sitting across from me.

'O'Keeffe — two e's and two f's,' he replied, 'Patrick Bede Xavier.'

The name rang a distant bell but I kept on with the paperwork, head bent down.

'Now Mary, your surname?' I asked, looking up at the heavily pregnant bride-to-be.

'O'Callaghan — Mary Therese Frances,' she replied quietly. Head still down, my brain was whirring; all this was ringing

179

as loudly as the Bells of St Clements but I just completed the paperwork and got on with the job.

And then it suddenly dawned on me.

This was *the* Father O'Keeffe who had knocked off Mary, the local Festival Queen and who had to leave town as quickly as he had been appointed to St Jude's. And here they were coming to get married in a civil ceremony.

God love 'em and bless 'em both.

Names never disappointed — and neither did poor, quiet, little John Thomas who resembled a jockey at the AJC and had a handshake like a dead fish and a personality to match. I guess the name had a huge bearing on his inability to perform or converse, let alone ride a winner at the Melbourne Cup.

Chapter 10
The Big Day

Names and lies. They all rear their ugly head even on the 'The Big Day' — the magic day everyone has been awaiting; the day the parents hand over their indulged, spoilt child for someone else to look after; the day which is supposed to dawn bright and clear, but sometimes it pees down buckets.

'Wendy,' wailed a bride on the phone. 'It's raining, what can you do about it?'

'Not my problem,' I felt like saying, 'Should I call the big fat pink fairy and see if she can stare into her crystal ball or wave her magic wand?'

But the 'The Big Day' dishes up its own wrath, despite every button, bow and bud which has been carefully organised and put in its place. There's nothing like sudden gusts of wind in the Southern Highlands: they are vicious to say the least and come when you least expect them.

It was Autumn on a cool Friday morning and as I looked at my watch to check the time, Moses tapped me on the shoulder.

'Wendy, I think it's going to rain before Rebecca arrives; what shall we do?'

'I think it'll hold off,' I told him, 'although the wind's getting up a bit; doesn't look good.'

Speak of the devil — an enormous gust of wind suddenly hit us right on the back and we both toppled slightly forward.

'Quick,' I called out to him, 'grab the chuppa!'

The Jewish chuppa had been beautifully decorated with fresh flowers but it had not been anchored into the lawn. It was just a decorated garden vine frame sitting on the grass.

Moses took an almighty dive at one of the legs of the frame but the wind tore it straight out of his hands, and as he fell forward onto the grass, the flowery frame went hurtling off towards the guests. Over and over it went, flowers and guests scattering.

David the best man, leaped into action grabbing the marriage wine decanter and silver goblets off the ceremony table, and clutching my briefcase and microphone, I ran for shelter towards the house, with a group of guests hanging on to their wigs and poor shaken Moses stumbling along beside me.

With flowers strewn from one end of the garden to the other it resembled the Royal Chelsea Flower Show. Guests shoved to get inside the house as though they were entering a football match, whilst a teary bride looked out glumly from the window of the bridal car, as it pulled up in the drive.

*　*　*

An old Greek father of the bride once said to me 'nothing's ever perfect' and this became my trusty motto for every wedding day especially when it came to the weather and especially in the Southern Highlands where the weather was even more unpredictable than the people.

Often when I asked who will hold and hand over the rings during the ceremony at the appointed time, I was told by the bride, 'Can't trust *him* bringing them. I'll put them down my bra so I know they're there.' But this practice is often not conducive to a smoothly-run ceremony.

With gloved hands, Stephanie was holding her flowers of the variety of exceptionally large lilies. It was almost impossible when the time came, for her other hand to reach down between

Chapter 10 — The Big Day

her breasts to find the rings, but on this occasion Craig came to the rescue by saying, 'Here lean over Steph; I'll get them.'

Again the photographer went into fast action as Craig plunged his right hand down between Steph's voluminous breasts, taking much longer than expected. But the rings were only in a small soft pouch and had slipped down around underneath the side of Steph's right breast, lodging right beneath her armpit. Craig had a further mission — to find the rings down Steph's breast but slightly to the right under the armpit, or else.

Of course by this time the guests were laughing and yelling out, 'Go for it, Craig,' and 'Watcha find there, Craig?' At last Craig located the rings around underneath Steph's armpit but Craig, being right-handed, found the whole extraction process even more difficult than plunging his hand down between Steph's breasts, in the first place.

With the rings finally produced from inside Steph's bridal bodice, the ceremony continued — except that firstly Steph had to prise off her wedding gloves after which Craig couldn't get the ring on Steph's finger because she was pregnant (and anyway, they were swollen in the heat of the day).

'Go on, push harder Craig, push harder,' she yelled at him so all the guests could hear.

'Yeah — push harder Craig!' yelled one of his mates.' Go for it Craigy, push mate!'

'Good honeymoon comin' up there Craigy,' yelled someone from the back row.

'Come on Craigy boy, push mate, push harder,' another piped up, until 120 guests were all yelling at Craig to 'push harder'.

Stephanie's mother, with her tiny fascinator bobbing up and down on the top of her head, was absolutely mortified and clearly the only one, not amused.

* * *

The Big Day

Anything can happen on 'The Big Day' — that's if the big day actually goes ahead after all the planning.

I had arrived in the local park and was setting up my P.A. System when my mobile went. 'Wendy!' screamed the bride. 'Len's gone missing; no-one can find him. No-one's seen him since last night. What'll we do?'

Asked when he was last seen, the bride told me that the night before was the 'buck's night' and Len and his mates had done a pub crawl that had commenced around five o'clock that afternoon. Around midnight having spent the past seven hours of solid drinking, they had pulled a prank on the groom in the carpark as they left. They had admitted to tying the groom's hands behind his back and his feet together before rolling him off the back of their ute, and he'd fallen into a ditch 'somewhere between Mittagong and Moss Vale.' I suggested she call the police, which meant delaying the wedding but there was nothing else anyone could do. Poor Len. They discovered him suffering from hypothermia still bound and lying in a one-metre ditch just below Mt Gibraltar near Mittagong. The wedding was postponed until the next day while poor Len recovered from his overnight ordeal. The bride and her family were far from impressed that their youngest daughter could even consider marrying such a person but she declared her undying love for him the next day despite poor Len being covered in cuts and bruises and nursing his very painful dislocated right shoulder in a sling.

* * *

Eyelashes too can be problematic and can have a habit of becoming unstuck especially when the emotional tears start to flow or the temperature is nearing 40 degrees.

Nicole's right eyelash decided to leave her eyelid in the middle of a stinking hot day; one half drooped down across the front of her eye while the other end stayed firmly glued in place.

Chapter 10 — *The Big Day*

'For Christ's sake, get rid of these fucking eyelashes, someone,' she whispered loudly trying not to blink them off. 'Bloody things,' she concluded looking across at me, blinking nineteen to the dozen.

Thankfully, the Matron of Honour came to her rescue. Passing her flowers to the bridesmaid to hold and with her back to the guests, she tried to pull off the remainder of Nicole's left eyelash — but it refused to budge.

'What'll I do?' she asked turning to me. 'It won't come off.'

I whispered to her, if she couldn't do it then neither could I.

We continued on with the ceremony with one half of Nicole's eyelash remaining firmly fixed in place and the other drooping down across the centre of her eye, while mascara dripped down her face and down between her breasts in the Summer heat.

* * *

Tired of looking single with the implications of 'not being able to find anyone', many brides felt being married made them rate higher in the popularity stakes and being 'Mrs' in name, had a certain mature ring to it.

Of course, some just wanted to be a princess for the day with all the attention being focussed upon them, some just wanted The Ring, while some just wanted to get pregnant so they didn't have to go back to work. Centrelink looked after many of these.

But all Toula had wanted was 'The Ring'. The Ring had become Toula's obsession. First and foremost Toula wanted to be married so she could have 'The Ring'. It was all she had ever talked about, her fascination for the jeweller's shop window had driven poor Michael crazy. He had told me all this, while waiting for her to arrive.

'If I hear about the bloody ring again,' moaned Michael, 'I'll kill 'er.'

The Big Day

Toula arrived at her ceremony early and as the ceremony dragged on, I noticed her eyes totally fixed on Little Uncle George seated in the front row. Waiting for The Ring was almost too much to bear, and the ceremony couldn't go quickly enough so that she could at last wear her chosen masterpiece. 'Little Uncle George' as she called him, was her favourite uncle, and being Toula's favourite, he had been given the all-important task of bringing the ring boxes forward for the happy couple at the appropriate time in the ceremony.

Toula had continually given him strict instructions about how it was to happen but poor Little Uncle George became a wreck over such a menial task. Even just thinking about it made his temperature rise. 'Bloody rings,' I had heard him mutter to someone before the ceremony.

Suddenly, it was ring time.

'Come on,' urged Toula holding her ring finger out, 'hurry up Uncle George; get the box open.'

Poor Little Uncle George fumbled and struggled with the fiddly, little ring box and finally managed to get his fat, stubby fingers with their bitten nails around the dainty little clip on the box. Toula with her ring finger poised up in the air for all to see the great moment of the ring actually being slipped on, trembled with sheer anticipation.

Her hand remained poised high in the air as poor Little Uncle George, leaned over the ring box and fumbled even more from sheer nervousness, trying to get the rings out. Little Uncle George was a short man of about 1.3 metres and of Greek descent with a nose that no others could beat. Its size and structure were of mammoth proportions and it hung off the front of his face like an enormous drooping chimney.

But Toula, in her haste and desperation to get the ring on her finger, pushed her finger further and further forward towards short Little Uncle George, calling, 'C'mon Uncle George hurry up! Get the ring out!' But as she continually urged him to hurry,

Chapter 10 — *The Big Day*

her finger kept getting higher in the air and closer and closer to poor Little Uncle George.

But as poor, short little Uncle George bent over the box to extract the rings, his large breathing apparatus got right in the way and Toula in the haste of thrusting her finger forward, pushed her ring finger right up Little Uncle George's generously large and inviting nose.

But because Little Uncle George was so short, Toula's finger bent backwards so it was stuck and it wasn't until Little Uncle George stood on tip-toes with his head tilted back and Toula twisted back her hand so that she could finally extract her ring finger from the massive chimney-like structure.

With a serious look, the photographer went into overdrive and clicked happily away; poor Little Uncle George, wiping the tears from his eyes, handed the groom Toula's ring. At last Toula felt married because she had The Ring but not before poor Little Uncle George had suffered his greatest indignity on such a special occasion.

* * *

I was often asked why I wear so many rings. Well, that's mainly because grooms have a habit of forgetting they are in the top drawer by the bed when they leave for the ceremony. Many a groom has left them tucked safely away at home. So I'm always on hand to lend a ring or two.

About to start a wedding, I had my usual quick little run-through with the groomsmen waiting for the bride to arrive. I'd check on the readers so they knew to come forward when asked and would show them how to hold the microphone — and then I'd check the groom had the rings.

'Jesus!' exclaimed Rodney. 'They're still in the drawer by the bed! She'll hold it against me for the rest of my life if I can't produce her ring.'

The Big Day

'How close by do you live?' I asked.

'Not far — quick, I'll be back before you know it.' The best man and the groom made a mad dash to the car.

Thankfully they got back with minutes to spare. 'But where's *your* ring?' I asked. 'You've got Mel's but who's got yours?'

'Mel's supposed to have mine; she didn't trust me with hers — funny if she forgot mine, then I'd really have something on her after all this time. Don't care if I get one or not,' he laughed.

Mel arrived swathed in the obligatory layers of white fluff but looking a million dollars. The bagpipers burst forth as Mel slid up the aisle.

'Bet she's forgotten it,' Rodney whispered winking across at me. 'Jeez I can't wait.'

Sure enough after all the hype and drama of the morning's activities, Mel failed to produce Rodney's ring and instead of being upset, he broke into peals of laughter. 'Gotcha at long last Mel, you'll never live this one down!'

And yet again, I lent one of my rings for the occasion.

* * *

But perhaps the worst ring scenario is when the best man, who generally has a habit of wanting to 'perform' when it's his turn to hand over the ring, likes pretending he'd forgotten them or pretending to drop them in the sand or in the grass. I quickly learned to tell them not to make a joke of handing over the rings, otherwise the bride would get upset 'and that's the last thing you'll want to live with,' I'd warn them. After 'the warning' I generally had no problems.

* * *

But this didn't stop a budding 'Marcel Marceau' who acted out his part like an Oscar Winning performer in the grounds of a Southern Highlands mansion.

'Marcel' had obviously been a student at NIDA and, with his bright carrot top hair, didn't disappoint. When I asked him to 'please hand over the rings' the act commenced and he leaped into action.

'Marcel' patted his jacket pockets and mimed a 'no' towards the guests, shaking his head from side to side. Then turning out his trouser pockets and finding nothing, again mimed a 'no' with facial expressions that would make a baby cry.

Then, a brain wave! 'Marcel's' eyes lit up and he reached inside his jacket pocket and produced a large oversized pink toy dummy. Again 'Marcel' shook his head from side to side. Thinking now, with his index finger under his chin and brows drawn together, he had one last inspiration. Eyes widened, he reached into another inside pocket and brought out his mobile phone. Again his head went from side to side, miming a 'no'.

By this time the guests were starting to make little groaning noises and with Mummy and Daddy waiting patiently on the lawn to see their dear daughter married off, 'Marcel' made his ultimate move. The rings! Ah yes, his eyes told the story. 'Marcel' did one final reach down the front of his trousers and produced the ring box from inside his daks.

But no one was amused, except poor pathetic 'Marcel' whose face broke into a large grin as he handed the rings across to the bride and groom. By this time the bride, was almost in tears and if looks could have killed, I would predict that 'Marcel' would never be spoken to again.

Their choice, I used to say to myself, they chose the stupid clown — not me. I took no delight in performing clowns who did nothing but upset an otherwise meaningful and sincere ceremony.

✳ ✳ ✳

But clowns and gymnasts in true form arrived at Athol Hall, Mosman, one day.

As the signing was taking place, the bride looked up and said, 'I have a surprise for you, Wendy.'

Nothing is worse than a surprise on a wedding day — ask any celebrant. A surprise generally indicates disaster as what a bride and groom may think is funny or entertaining, can often spell chaos or disaster.

But this surprise was truly delightful and just as the final congratulations were being offered, a colourful band of clowns and gymnasts came running and rolling out onto the lawn performing a myriad of tricks and treats. I'd have chosen these colourful clowns any day of the week rather than 'Marcel', the NIDA trained goose.

* * *

But 'The Big Day' wouldn't be 'The Big Day' without the Mother of the Bride swanning around in all her glory. Some of them came dressed to kill — often their well-chosen fascinators outshone the boring bridal veils. But, it seemed, the larger the fascinator, the better.

Serena's mother had hired the biggest and the best yacht for her 80 exclusive hand-picked guests and wearing the obligatory monster fascinator upon her carefully coiffured hair and heels as high as a baby stork's legs, she greeted everyone with a loose little handshake. Her low-cut designer frock would have put the Melbourne Cup 'Fashions on the Field' to shame. Mother had paid for everything, nothing had been forgotten — no holds barred and the Moet flowed freely.

A perfectly written ceremony was well underway and as we came to the vows, I asked the groom to repeat the words they had chosen. But halfway through repeating the vows the groom stopped and spun around saying, 'Wendy, these aren't the vows I

Chapter 10 — *The Big Day*

chose.' I quietly hastened to remind him they were exactly what the bride had emailed me the week prior to the wedding after they had visited to practice.

'They are not,' insisted the groom starting to raise his voice. 'These aren't what we chose at Wendy's place,' he accused, turning towards his wife-to-be.

'Oh shut up,' interjected the bride standing there in all her glory. 'Just say them and just shut up.'

'I will *not* say them,' replied the groom angrily. 'These vows are *not* what I chose when we practiced. You have gone and changed them.'

'For God's sake shut up,' the bride hissed. 'The ones you chose were total crap. Mother and I chose these and they're exactly what you're going to say, so get on with it.'

With that, the groom pulled his hands out of hers and yelled, 'Well that's it then. You can shove your fucking wedding up your tight little fucking arse and drop me back at the wharf!'

Refusing to be calmed down by the bride, the groom, his best men, the photographer and I were all dropped back at the wharf and the bride-to-be sailed away into the sunset with Mother, to party with the 80 astounded guests.

* * *

And so from crises to the adventurous — I was amazed that the couple about to be married had decided on an area right beside children's swings and slides. This will be interesting, I thought, but at least sensible. The children could have some fun as the adults enjoyed the solemnity of the wedding — at least these kids could amuse themselves instead of display the usual whinging and whining one normally encounters.

But the true meaning of choosing this location became much clearer as I declared the happy couple 'husband and wife', as after they had both kissed to seal their union and with a sparkle in their

191

The Big Day

eyes and a knowing look between themselves, the bride hitched up her skirts and off they took up to the top of the Flying Fox landing, where they both grabbed the ropes and took an almighty leap.

With one tremendous heave on the ropes, the two beautifully wedding-clad bodies of the bride and groom swung down over the top of the guests.

To me, the bride resembled the Flying Nun in a pure white habit as she flew through the air with the greatest of ease, with the groom sailing high behind her in full flight.

Now if anything brightens my day, it's the thought of the Flying Nun being pursued by a randy Tarzan mid-air, both in full bridal regalia.

* * *

Occasionally if the couple were religious but didn't want the fuss and bother of the church wedding, or having to promise to adhere to the church's doctrines and rules, they would choose me as their celebrant and invite their local parish priest to bless the rings or offer a blessing at the end of the ceremony.

Amanda's parish priest was none other than the larger than life figure of Father O'Neill who turned up with a whiskey or three under his belt reeking with its very smell — but then, everyone's entitled to a few drinks on a wedding day.

But it's not such a good idea if consumed prior to the ceremony rather than afterwards, especially if it's the frustrated and sermon-loving parish priest.

However, a few sherbets at the Presbytery had turned Father O'Neill into a talkative Red-rumped Parrot. He went on and on, about the sanctity of marriage and the attributes of a perfect relationship, even threatening the couple that 'divorce between Catholic couples was still and would probably always be alive and well'.

Poor Amanda and Christopher, their ceremony marred by the word 'divorce' wiped the smiles off their faces, but the larger

Chapter 10 — *The Big Day*

than life Father O'Neill made no apologies for his sermon. He just couldn't help himself. After about 30 minutes expounding the vices and virtues of matrimony, he finally finished and as I was declaring the astounded couple 'husband and wife', out the corner of my eye I could see the blessed Father heading for the bar.

From one chalice to another, so very blessed indeed. The good Father's prayers were generally answered on wedding days.

* * *

And from one extreme to the other. Basil wanted the minimum amount of fuss, no religious blessing for him — just the basics, he told me on the phone. Barbara just went along with what he wanted — a small and intimate wedding in the local park.

'We're just having five guests,' he confided. 'No reception; maybe just some chips and dips afterwards to celebrate.'

'Fair enough,' I reassured them. 'Do exactly as you want on your wedding day.'

The ceremony was short but Basil seemed happy enough. Then he made an announcement.

'Over this way everyone, let's celebrate.'

Basil made a beeline for the Eski and reaching in, pulled out one little plastic carton of avocado dip and one small packet of chicken-flavoured chips. Then reaching into the Eski again, out came a couple of old kitchen glasses and a couple of pre-used Vegemite jars which he promptly filled with some good old el cheapo cardboard cantata.

'Doesn't matter if these break,' he announced, 'we can just throw them away. OK — here's cheers to us!'

None of us knew which way to look, and as I headed off to my next wedding I decided it was no wonder he was already 53 and had 'Never Validly Married'.

* * *

193

The Big Day

Wine was occasionally the order of 'The Big Day' and couples celebrated 'Sharing of the Wine' during the ceremony. It's great if the bottle's screw-topped but not so great if one needs a cork screw which neither Brendan nor the blushing bride had thought to bring. So while the beautiful crystal goblets sparkled in the Australian sunlight, Brendan took off by car to the nearest pub to see if they'd lend him a corkscrew.

So with half of the ceremony completed we could do nothing more but wait until Brendan returned. And wait we all did, under the motley shade of a few gum trees in the Royal Botanic Gardens, as the sun beat down.

Finally an exhausted Brendan and his best man came racing back with the obligatory corkscrew. Brendan wrenched out the cork, poured some wine for the bride and him, and linking arms they repeated their vows.

Need I say that the remainder of the wine was finished off by the guests who passed the bottle around amongst themselves while the Marriage Register was being signed? Drinking straight from the bottle, they toasted the happy couple while the photographer captured some brilliant candid pics.

* * *

But sometimes 'The Big Day' doesn't arrive after all the finest of preparations and thousands of dollars spent. Sitting in my office the day before Angela's wedding was due to take place, I answered the phone.

'It's the Colonel here, Wendy,' said a toffy voice. 'Thought I'd better inform you the wedding's off — the bloody little bastard's done a bunker.'

Angela was a gorgeous girl and David a good-looking young man. They came to me with the inevitable stars in their eyes.

They were to marry on her parents' front lawn in front of one of the most majestic homes I'd been to. No expense had been

Chapter 10 — *The Big Day*

spared for the only daughter's marriage — the marquee was up, the truckloads of flowers and champagne and ceremonial requirements were all ready — except for David who, under the watchful eye of The Colonel and his wife, could no longer stand the whole wedding spectacular and had buckled beneath its very pressure.

So not having had to put his hand in his pocket for one solitary item of the wedding expense apart from Angela's engagement and wedding rings, and with nothing to lose except his dignity, he had raced to the airport and jumped on the first available flight back to New Zealand.

The Colonel I think, was probably rather relieved that his dear little Amanda could now settle for someone more suitable, so it wasn't with too much remorse from his end of the phone that he'd announced 'the little bastard had done a bunker'.

The Colonel's wife promptly bundled the distraught Angela onto the next flight to Rome so she could recover from the nasty shock of David's disappearance back to New Zealand and I believe the champagne was not wasted the next day. Apparently, the Colonel invited as many of his old cronies and neighbours as he could get in touch with, and devouring the kilos of smoked salmon, caviar and every delicious tit-bit, they drank themselves into oblivion until the sun came up and every last drop was gone.

Dream on beautiful bride … nothing's ever perfect, as much as you'd like it to be and a bride seldom takes advice from a celebrant, however well-meaning.

* * *

Fluttering butterflies are another big dream but dreams don't always come true on 'The Big Day'. Butterflies don't always fly and can't be told what to do and generally end their delicate little lives breathing their last, smothered inside a butterfly box, long before it's opened at the appropriate time.

The Big Day

Sally told me excitedly, 'We're having butterflies as you declare us "husband and wife".'

I just smiled and said, 'That's nice Sally; they'll look good in the photos.' But I'd experienced all this many times before.

The temperatures were in the high 30s as we stood in the insufferable heat and the flies stuck to us like glue; the Australian wave was going full bore. Eventually after a full-on ceremony with three readings and Celtic handfasting, I declared the lovely Sally and her groom, 'husband and wife'.

Right on cue, the butterfly lady ran forward with her open box of butterflies, blowing furiously to make the butterflies take flight. But the whole box of butterflies had suffocated to death — not a single one had survived to flutter forth to delight the eyes of the bride or the children and the waiting photographer.

All the children started crying to see the little dead butterflies except young eight-year-old Samuel who did not miss his big moment but ran around fervently gathering them all up.

'Look Mum,' he called opening his hands to show her all the dead butterflies, 'we can take these home for Scottie!'

'Scottie's a dog, Samuel; he won't eat dead butterflies,' she told him.

'Yes he will Mum. He'll be hungry by the time we get back.'

'No Samuel, go and bury them in the garden. I'm not taking that dog of yours dead butterflies home for dinner,' replied his mother.

So I knelt down in my best wedding attire and helped Samuel dig a little hole in which to bury the dead butterflies as Sally dried her tears, but not before I saw Samuel stuff three dead ones into the pocket of his pants. Of course I pretended not to see a thing.

* * *

Chapter 10 — *The Big Day*

I learned not to say how nice butterflies look in the photos because seldom have I ever seen a photo with a butterfly in it, well — not a live one, anyway. Emily told me they were having butterflies as well, so I just smiled but then couldn't resist saying, 'They don't normally live in the heat, Emily. They usually die in the box beforehand.'

'Ours will be OK,' she replied. 'Anyway, I've already paid for them.'

Dream on beautiful bride, I thought, don't listen to me.

Of course on the day, again another insufferable Sydney hot one, the box revealed eight dozen dead butterflies which just flopped down to the ground as the butterfly lady blew them out of the box.

'You told me that would happen, Wendy,' said Emily wistfully. 'I won't have them next time.'

'There'd bloody better not be a next time,' snapped the groom, 'especially at spending eight dollars each — and you went and ordered eight bloody dozen for good luck.'

I quickly worked out that the butterflies had cost more than I had charged; as usual the couple placed little importance on the legal and ceremonial aspect — it was all about the big meringue, the butterflies and the champagne.

* * *

Once, but only once, did one or two butterflies, which fluttered around hopelessly after their release, live to tell the tale, only to get lost in the strange environment and end their short-lived lives there and then because the hungry waiting currawongs perched above took just a few seconds to swoop down and devour the tasty little morsels. That was the end of that. A tasty entrée for any keen and hungry currawong.

* * *

When the word doves are mentioned I also go into overdrive with a bit of advice. 'They'll circle around above us and probably poo over all the guests,' I warn the bride.

'Not at our wedding they won't,' replied the confident Bernie. 'My uncle's letting us use some of his homing pigeons for the day. They're well-trained, you know.'

But poo the pigeons did, right across the suited shoulder of the best man and Bernie's mother as they set off on their homeward bound journey above us, and not before Bernie's poor mother Janine burst into loud sobs.

'This is just too awful,' she cried trying to wipe pigeon poo of her left shoulder. 'We had doves at my mother's funeral and this reminds me of the ones we had there.' With that, both Janine's sisters also burst into loud sobs and with their comforting arms around each other, headed off towards the chilled champagne.

* * *

Another non-wedding day; a day before the prearranged wedding day and I still hadn't heard from the bride and groom who were supposed to have arrived from the UK a week before. With neither the final paperwork nor ceremony typing done, my roadie called her number.

'Hello, this is the celebrant's office here — Wendy's your marriage celebrant,' he started. 'Is that Joy?'

'Yes,' slurred a voice.

'One moment Joy and I'll hand you over to Wendy.'

As I said, 'Hello Joy,' the phone went mysteriously dead. So I called the photographer who lived just a block from where she was supposed to be staying and obligingly, he took time to go around and 'suss out' the situation.

But no-one answered the door — no sign of life.

I left numerous phone messages and eventually sent an email asking her to contact me urgently otherwise I would be unable

Chapter 10 — *The Big Day*

to perform the ceremony. So with the Royal Botanic Gardens booked and both the photographer's and my deposits paid, that was the last we ever heard from Joy.

No apologetic phone call, no explanation, no email, no nothing.

The least anyone can do is to contact the celebrant to say that the wedding's off. I have never heard from them from that day to this, sometimes 'The Big Day' is a fizzer and just doesn't go ahead at all.

* * *

Birds also have a lot to do with weddings and I don't mean those of the human female variety. Anne and Will's wedding was to be a very solemn occasion — everything had to be just right and had been meticulously planned. The couple had travelled from Scotland and I had been given strict instructions about the organisational process of the day, as many friends and family were flying into Sydney from all around the globe.

I had organised three bagpipers to pipe in the happy couple, but I wasn't aware that kookaburras just love the sound of bagpipes and are more than happy to compete with their bloodcurdling wail. Just as Anne and Will started to repeat their vows, a flock of laughing kookaburras sitting right above us in a Ghost Gum tree started their traditional kookaburra 'hoo-hoo-hoo ha-ha-ha' laugh.

They chortled and laughed, laughed and chortled the whole way through the remainder of the ceremony much to the delight of the overseas jet-lagged guests who ended up with their eyes focussed up in the heights of the gum tree taking photographs instead of concentrating on the all-important seriousness of the occasion and taking photos of the bride.

After all, it was *her* Big Day.

'Oh shut up,' yelled Anne brushing back her veil, squinting up at the kookaburras. But the kookaburras just seemed to laugh even louder as Anne went redder in the face. 'You've spoilt my whole wedding day; sod off you bloody Australian kookaburras,' she cried.

'Anne,' I said thinking very quickly, as she signed the Marriage Register, 'kookaburras are a great sign of good luck on a wedding day here in Australia. It's an Australian thing.'

'Oh really?' enquired Anne looking up at the chortling birds. 'Well in that case …'

But too late. One old grandfather of a kookaburra suddenly let rip and did an almighty poo right on the top of Anne's veil.

'See,' I said smiling, 'now you've got double good luck!'

But I'm not sure whether Anne was fully convinced about that one. As the poor groom tried to wipe the sticky mess from her veil and hair, with his pocket handkerchief, the horrified look on her face said it all.

I don't think Anne believed a word I'd said, and I couldn't blame her. It was probably one of the biggest fibs I had ever told but it sounded convincing at the time and I *had* to say something to save The Big Day.

* * *

Another bird, which seems to love a wedding or two, is the Wonga pigeon which is famous for its high-pitched 'coo-coo', especially in mating season when this tiring call comes with monotonous regularity every couple of seconds or so, and just doesn't let up. They call and call until a mate responds.

These can be a real nuisance if you're in a bushland area such as a National Park and nothing in the world will make them go away — even a solitary bagpiper couldn't move this bird because it just continuously goes on and on with its 'coo-coo, coo-coo, coo-coo' trying to reach a suitable mate who'll respond in the same tiresome way.

'What on earth's that bloody bird?' asked a guest, looking up.

Chapter 10 — *The Big Day*

'It's a Wonga pigeon,' I replied. 'It's their mating season. Look there it is — you can just see its spotty white breast.'

'I'll give it bloody Wonga pigeon,' replied Aaron the best man and suddenly disappeared through the bush track over towards his ute.

It wasn't long before Aaron returned — this time with a .303 rifle — and taking careful aim and with one pull of the trigger, the rifle kicking back against his shoulder, Aaron blasted the poor Wonga pigeon off its perch — a mass of blood, guts and feathers shattering like a crystal glass against a marble floor, and a bunch of dumbstruck guests ducking for cover.

'That'll teach the bastard,' gloated Aaron.' Better put this back in the car before Jilly arrives.'

But as predicted, the local ranger arrived at the rate of knots just before Jilly and her bridesmaids, and leaning out of his truck window asked whether the shooting noise had come from over our way.

We were all still so dumb-struck we just nodded our heads saying, 'No — didn't come from over this way,' as a smiling Aaron came sauntering back through the undergrowth.

* * *

But trust the poor Kiwi parents to get it so wrong, on 'The Big Day' — 'specially Lana's. 'Mum and Dad are coming over from Auckland,' the bride told me at our first meeting. 'Glad you were born there Wendy, Mum isn't that keen on Aussies. Anyway, quite a few rellies are coming over the ditch for the wedding. Most haven't been here before, so this'll be the big experience for them,' she concluded.

'I'm not much of a Kiwi these days, Lana,' I told her. 'I'm an Aussie; been here for years.'

'That's OK,' said Lana. 'Mum's still getting used to the fact that I took out Aussie citizenship last year. Don't worry; she'll love you! Nothing like a Kiwi in her books!'

Lana and Ian decided beautiful McKell Park at Darling Point was the ideal spot for their Big Day and everything was set to roll when my mobile went.

'Wendy, it's Lana,' came the familiar voice. 'Are Mum and Dad there yet? I don't want to arrive before they do. We're in the limo just coming up New South Head Road — Dad's giving me away.' But there had been no sign of Lana's parents.

'OK, I'll call them on their mobile,' said Lana as she hung up.

The next minute, Lana called again. 'Wendy, I've just spoken to Mum and Dad and they've gone and got bloody lost. They've gone and hired a fucking car and can't find fucking McKell Park. Can you fucking believe it? I told them just to take a cab — they're only staying up in College Street. Listen, I'll get the limo driver to see if he can find them and then they can follow us back to McKell.'

A whole hour later and with melting Kiwis waiting in mid-30 degree heat, Lana was on the phone again, hysterical this time.

'Where on earth are you, Lana?' I asked. 'Everyone's dying in this heat.'

'Fuck my stupid fucking parents,' screamed back Lana. 'They missed the fucking turnoff in New South Head Road and ended up right out at fucking Watsons Bay. Can you fucking believe it! You just can't trust them one little bit. Anyway,' she continued, 'we found them out near The Gap and they're following us back now. We're as far back as Elizabeth Bay … won't be long.'

Eventually, the stretch limo with the irate Lana and her three bridesmaids arrived at snail's pace down Darling Point Road, and having finished off almost all the freebie champagne provided by the limo people, the bridesmaids emerged from the car in high spirits, just as Lana's frustrated parents pulled up behind.

Chapter 10 — *The Big Day*

But Lana, not one for mincing her words, and not waiting for the photographer to get the all-important 'smiling-bride-hanging-out-of-the-limo-window' shots, she jumped out and hitching up her voluminous skirts, raced back over to her parents' car.

'You are both just fucking idiots,' she screamed at them through the car window. 'You hire a fucking car in a fucking city you've never fucking been to before … you miss the fucking turn-off which is just up the fucking road from where you're fucking staying, and you end up out at fucking Watsons Bay. Now just fuck off the pair of you. I wish I'd never fucking invited you over to the fucking wedding in the first fucking place.'

The still very much sober Lana who had been on her mobile phone most of the way out to Watsons Bay and back didn't stop for a breath and turning to her father screamed, 'And you can fuck off too. You are not going to fucking give me away, and that's fucking that.'

With such a berating from their dearly loved, one and only daughter, Lana's mum and dad burst into tears as my roadie quietly escorted them across to the ceremony area, while Lana tried to compose herself — skirts up in one hand and a hardly touched bottle of champagne in the other.

As Lana took a swig of champagne straight from the bottle down her overworked throat, she turned to the limo driver and let out one final stream of abuse.

'And fuck you too,' she screamed as a parting shot. 'You drive too fucking slow for such a large fucking car. And there wasn't even enough fucking champagne for four fucking people.'

The partially pissed and giggling bridesmaids who were falling all over themselves, headed off towards the garden's gates, totally ignoring the raging Lana who was trying to straighten down her dress with one hand, still firmly clutching her nearly full bottle with the other.

But the three giggling bridesmaids who weren't in the mood to offer Lana any help with her dress, didn't escape a final berating. Adding a few more words that rhymed with 'hunt' and 'hole' from her repertoire, Lana handed the bottle to me, smoothed down her skirts as best she could in readiness to follow the staggering bridesmaids up the aisle, and turning to me as though butter wouldn't melt in her mouth, she smiled sweetly and said, 'Hi Wendy, thank God I've got you here to keep me calm — now let's get this fucking show on the road.'

I hadn't uttered a word the whole time and with my roadie Philip, who had returned after going back to the limo to calm the driver down, I commenced proceedings. I think I recall smiling through the whole ceremony — Lana was so good for the soul. How I wish half of them could have been as honest as her and said exactly what they thought.

*　*　*

It wasn't long after Lana's wedding that I heard about 'The Shortest Fairy Tale in the World'.

'You see,' slurred an alcoholic Father of the Bride, spitting right into my face and peering down the top of my bra, 'once upon a time, a man asked his girlfriend, "Will you marry me?"

'She said, "No."

And so the man lived happily ever after.'

*　*　*